the

CUP

of

OUR LIFE

the

CUP

of

OUR LIFE

———◆❧◆———

a guide to spiritual growth

JOYCE RUPP

SORIN BOOKS  Notre Dame, Indiana

Scripture quotations are from the *New Revised Standard Version* of the Bible, copyright © 1993 and 1989 by the Division of Christian Education of the National Council of Churches of Christ in the USA. Used by permission. All rights reserved.

Excerpt from *Gitanjali: A Collection of Indian Songs* by Rabindranath Tagore (New York: Macmillan, 1971) is reprinted with permission of Simon and Schuster.

Excerpt from "Landscape" is taken from *Dream Work*, copyright © 1986 by Mary Oliver. Used by permission of Grove Atlantic, Inc.

Excerpts from *Open Secret: Versions of Rumi*, copyright © 1984 by John Moyne and Coleman Barks, are used by permission of Threshold Books, Putney, VT.

Excerpt from *Psalms of Lament* by Ann Weems is used by permission of Westminster John Knox Press, Louisville, KY.

Excerpts from *Selected Poetry of Jessica Powers*, Regina Siegfried and Robert Morneau, eds., are reprinted with permission of Sheed and Ward, 115 East Armour Blvd. Kansas City, MO 64111.

Excerpt from "You Are a Love Song" by Theresa Hucal is taken from *Harvesting: Songs of Theresa Hucal*, copyright © 1987, The Sisters of Charity, New Brunswick, Canada. Used by permission.

Excerpts from *The Way of Passion: A Celebration of Rumi*, copyright © 1986 by Andrew Harvey, are reprinted by permission of Frog, Ltd., PO Box 2327, Berkeley, CA 94712.

Founded in 1865, Ave Maria Press is a ministry of the United States Province of Holy Cross.

www.avemariapress.com

Paperback ISBN-10 1-933495-31-6 ISBN-13 978-1-933495-31-6

Ebook ISBN-10 1-933495-53-7 ISBN-13 978-1-933495-53-8

Cover image ©Thinkstock.

Cover and text design by Brian C. Conley.

Illustrations © Jane Pitz 2012.

Printed and bound in the United States of America.

Library of Congress Cataloging-in-Publication Data
    Rupp, Joyce.
    The cup of our life : a guide for spiritual growth / Joyce Rupp ; illustrations by Jane Pitz.
    p. cm.
    Includes bibliographical references.
ISBN 0-87793-625-0. — ISBN 0-87793-626-9 (alk. paper)
1. Devotional calendars. I. Title.
BV4811.R76 1997
    242'.2—dc21
    97-19768
    CIP

For all those

who have been with me

when we have prayed with a cup.

Together we have brought

this book to birth.

This cup holds grief and balm

in equal measure, light, darkness.

Who drinks from it must change.

—MAY SARTON

CONTENTS

PREFACE

The other day I was in a hurry and broke the handle off my favorite coffee cup by carelessly hitting it on the sink. This large cup with delicate purple and blue flowers has a thin rim that makes drinking from it "just perfect." When it broke, I thought, "This is a bit ironic, breaking my beloved cup in the midst of writing the preface to *The Cup of Our Life*."

I felt irritated at myself for such mindless behavior and sad to have caused that damage. I recognized in this experience how much a cup can take on a life of its own. This cup had accompanied me every morning after my meditation and journal writing and often for evening tea. Yesterday I found some strong glue, and now the handle is again firmly attached. As I look at the cup this morning, the cracks in the mended part remind me of the flaw in myself that tends to rush too much.

A cup can evoke a compelling connection with one's self. I learned this in the twenty years since *The Cup of Our Life* was first published. While I enjoyed creating this book, I had considerable mistrust and apprehension about its ability to speak to those who used it. I wasn't sure others would find the potential for spiritual growth that I did in the cup's symbolism. As it turned out, this concern of mine was wasted energy.

During the years after *The Cup of Our Life* emerged, I received countless messages from readers telling me how profoundly their encounter with the cup imagery changed their lives. These messages have never stopped coming.

Hearing these stories renews my strong belief in the power of symbol to connect our worldly selves to our deeper soul-selves. It is in this connection that we can find meaning and inspiration to live more fully.

Not long ago one of my readers reminisced in a letter and reminded me of a retreat I had given. Judie's comment re-confirmed how this movement from the exterior to the interior of our lives takes place when we pause to pray with a symbol:

> You invited each of us to bring a cup and introduce ourselves to each other by sharing a story of the cup's significance. That retreat awakened me into the ordinary experiences of life that are made holy when seen through the eyes of faith. Praying with our cups during that week of retreat set me on a path of appreciation for all the simple things of life that bring the sacred home to me. I return to this book over and over during times of difficulty or transition in my life.

It is not so much that our lives are made holy by symbolism. Rather, symbols invite us to go beyond our obscured and tired views, to enter the hidden dimensions inherent in our lives and to refresh our awareness of the sacred. Most recently at a conference, an older woman whose family had been killed in the Holocaust came to me with *The Cup of Our Life* in her hands. With moist eyes, she held it out and said, "This is exactly what I need now, especially the cup of blessing. It is time for me to look beyond my sorrow and see what is of value in my life."

Those who have experienced life's woundedness and troubled events are especially influenced by the various imageries associated with the cup. This is another power of symbolism. It can move us to a place where we find our unique experience connected to the universal experience of others. When this happens, it can bring both comfort and strength. Geraldine expressed this well when she wrote from Ireland about using the book: "In essence we all go through similar stuff at different times in our lives."

Her comment is reflected in that of Marci, another correspondent:

> I am writing to let you know how much *The Cup of Our Life* has meant to me over the years. The first time I went through the book . . . my mother was dying of cancer, my daughter was struggling with health issues, and my husband was going through a career transition. I experienced a tremendous sense of loneliness

and despair during that time, but the one thing that I looked forward to each morning was getting my cup and notepad out and reading from *The Cup of Our Life*. It was like someone opened a window and let fresh air into my soul. I took courage from the readings and began to develop a prayer life that continues to sustain me today. I'm happy to say that I made it through that tough time and have come out of it with a greater appreciation for developing my spiritual life.

Knowing that this book has helped another person to develop or sustain a prayer life lifts my heart. Others have expressed similar comments, like Gale's note: "I read *The Cup of Our Life* and learned to pray. When I finished the six week program, I went back, read, and prayed with it again. . . . I had found myself in a spiritual wasteland until the book made me feel human and normal. *The Cup of Our Life* opened up a pathway to God for me."

People of various ages from different countries have let me know how this book influenced their lives. From newly married couples and college and seminary students, to medical personnel and elderly folks, I continue to learn of their spiritual growth when they pay attention to how a cup speaks to them. One of the most moving stories I heard regarding this book came while I was visiting a prison in Ohio. The chaplain invited me to come and sit in a circle of incarcerated women who had read and prayed with *The Cup of Our Life*. As the women shared about their study, I was touched by their depth of insight and their desire for personal transformation. Later the chaplain described the experience of an inmate with cancer who had been part of this group. When the cancer became terminal, she was moved to a hospice facility. As she was preparing to leave the prison, the only thing this dying woman asked to take with her was the cup she had chosen and prayed with for six weeks.

I have also appreciated learning about the kinds of cups readers choose to use for their prayer journeys. Helen described meditating on what kind of cup she was:

> My thoughts kept going to my girlfriend who would have chosen a fine thin white porcelain cup and saucer. I, on the other hand, felt like a worn piece of stoneware maybe with a chip or two. I questioned why I couldn't be the beautiful cup. *The Cup of Our Life* spoke to me: I was reachable, approachable, not a cup to be put on a shelf and admired. I realized people would talk to me,

tell me about themselves because I was open to them. Perhaps the worn-ness and chips of my life reminded others of the harmony of our imperfect humanness.

When I designed this book, I did so with the hope that not only individuals would find it helpful but also that groups who were seeking to enhance and deepen their faith life could use it. Fortunately, this occurred. Claudia wrote from Colorado to tell me she was "profoundly affected" by the chapter on the "The Perfect Cup." This led to Claudia's facilitation of days of reflection on perfectionism. Along with this, she used the sections on "The Chipped Cup" and "The Broken Cup" to lead "forgiveness" retreats and seminars. Her latest project is to develop a spiritual formation experience around chapter five, "The Cup of Compassion."

A deacon named Patrick and his wife gathered some of their friends in Massachusetts. They read the book and shared their reflections on it, their cups, and their lives. Patrick wrote to say thanks and added: "It gave us all something to take with us, to look at and into, as an example of what we do in our sharing of faith." Similarly, Sara, a young high school campus minister, used the book with a faculty group. Another woman mentioned she had "participated in this book three times, once with a close friend, once with a group of women, and once with a group of college friends" and that each time the cup revealed new things to her.

Something I did not fully anticipate is how rich and enduring the bonds would be among those who prayed with *The Cup of Our Life*. People who were acquaintances became friends. Those who were friends grew deeper in their relationships. Married couples learned to see each other in a fresh light.

The union of faith among those using the book goes further than one of lingering enjoyment. It often provides much needed courage in times of adversity. Such has been the situation with a Nova Scotia group from the United Church of Canada. Karen described how they "embarked on a journey, meeting weekly to share emotional stories of our lives as symbolized by the cup. . . . We quickly created a bond so strong that when three of our members went through major back surgery, a brain tumor, and a brain aneurysm in the next year we drew on our closeness, our new understanding, and our support for one another to sustain us."

Another aspect I did not consider is that readers might repeatedly use the book and have a different choice of cup each time. I discovered this from Jeanne who told me that her cups included a rustic clay mug she made in a pottery class in high school and a china cup with yellow roses and butterflies. Not only that, Jeanne also surprised me when she told me she has given *The Cup of Our Life* as a gift many times, sometimes with a cup she selects for the recipient. Jeanne described the kind she gives: "It might be re-gifting a cup I have used and found revealing in my meditations. Sometimes for someone who has used the book before, if I find a special cup that suits them, I'll suggest they read the book again with this new cup."

And so, God has once more surprised me, going far beyond my hopes for this book, taking what was given to me and growing it into something much larger. I find this response both humbling and gratifying. I hope a similar sort of spiritual enrichment happens for you, dear readers and seekers, as you enter *The Cup of Our Life*.

ACKNOWLEDGMENTS

This book has within it the touch of many people. Participants at my workshops, retreats, and conferences continually added gems of creative insight and awareness as we used the cup as a symbol of our spiritual life. I carry the presence of these people with me as I recall how enriching the writing of this book has been.

How thankful I am for the day when Norm Litzner invited Richard Rehfeldt and me to pray with the cup. That was the graced moment when the idea of this book was first conceived. Both of these co-pastors have been very attentive to their own spiritual journeys, and they have greatly blessed mine.

Judy Cauley's fingerprints are all over this book. She reviewed the completed manuscript and offered many energizing suggestions to improve the text and the prayers.

Several groups journeyed together with the manuscript for six weeks. They not only prayed with the cup each day, they also gave me detailed evaluations for what did and did not help them as they prayed. My thanks for their ideas and especially for their vulnerability in allowing me into their prayer life. I am very grateful to these pray-ers: Janet Barnes, Lisa Brandser, Betty Honz, Joyce Hutchison, Mark Lindahl, Joan McLaughlin, Dee Malena-Polosky, Mike Polosky, Jean Smith, Cathy Talarico, and Vicki Vanderkwaak.

I thank publisher Frank Cunningham, editor Robert Hamma, and artist Jane Pitz for their careful and thorough help as we worked together on readying the manuscript for publication. I am also aware of all those who work "behind the scenes." This is my fourth book with Ave Maria Press, and I continue to be astounded at both the efficiency and the care with which the books are marketed and mailed.

This book would never have come to life without the woman who gave me birth: Hilda Wilberding Rupp. Her zest for life and her positive approach to each day have been wonderful sources of encouragement for me.

As I reflect on all who have helped the book to take life, I am grateful for those who walk closely with me in my life: friends, family, and my religious community, the Servants of Mary. Because of them my cup of blessing is often filled to the brim.

INTRODUCTION

I remember vividly the day I first began pondering the cup as a symbol of my inner journey. It happened on a Wednesday morning as I sat down for a regularly scheduled midweek prayer with the two co-pastors of Windsor Heights Lutheran Church. On that particular morning, Norm had asked Dick and me to bring our empty coffee mugs to prayer. As we settled in, Norm invited us to hold our cups, to look into them, and to think about our spiritual lives. At that moment, the symbolism of the cup awakened me to the deeper part of myself.

What happened was amazing. I had no sooner looked into the empty cup when tears began forming in my eyes. What was this about? Why this great surge of sadness? Where did this deep emotion come from? As I struggled with my tears and continued looking into the empty cup, I discovered that I was feeling much more spiritually drained than I had realized. Looking into the empty cup was like looking into my hollow self.

Since that time I have found the cup to be a powerful teacher for my inner life. The ordinariness of the cup reminds me that my personal transformation occurs in the common crevices of each day. The cup is an apt image for the inner processes of growth. The cup has been a reminder of my spiritual thirst. As I've held it, filled it, drunk from it, emptied it and washed it, I've learned that it is through my ordinary human experiences that my thirst for God is quenched. In the cup I see life, with its emptiness, fullness, brokenness, flaws, and blessings.

A cup is a container for holding something. Whatever it holds has to eventually be emptied out so that something more can be put into it. I have learned that I cannot always expect my life to be full. There has to be some emptying, some pouring out, if I am to make room for the new. The spiritual journey is like that—a constant process of emptying and filling, of giving and receiving, of accepting and letting go.

The cup has taught me many valuable lessons for my spiritual growth. I have learned that my life holds stale things that need to be discarded, and that sometimes my life feels as wounded as a broken cup. I have learned that I have flaws, chips, and stains, just as any well-used cup may have, but that these markings of a well-traveled life need not prevent me from being a valuable gift for others. I have learned that the contents of my life are meant to be constantly given and shared in a generous gesture of compassion, just as the main purpose of a cup is to have its contents given away. I have especially learned gratitude for all those moments when the unexpected has transformed my life into an abundant cup of blessings.

Notice the rim on a cup. It is circular, with no beginning or end, a symbol of wholeness. In the circle all is connected to form a oneness. The spiritual life is a journey toward becoming whole, a day-to-day movement of continually growing into the person we are meant to be. The cup's rim or circle daily reminds me of this longing for wholeness and connectedness.

This yearning for greater spiritual oneness with God is the foundation of *The Cup of Our Life*. I hope that this six-week guide, which is centered around the many facets of a cup, will inspire you to grow in your relationship with God and will fill your cup of life to overflowing.

As You Begin the Journey

The spiritual life is a journey about change. As you pray with the cup, you will undoubtedly experience opportunities for growth. These stirrings may be almost imperceptible or they may be very noticeable. There is no "goal" that you have to meet as you pray through the weeks. Simply be open and allow yourself to be held in the shelter of God. Also allow yourself to be stretched a bit. You may find, at times, that your security is being challenged, that your rootedness in God is being drawn to depths you've not experienced before, or that your approach to life is being taken to the edge of your comfort zone. If this happens, please don't run away from the edge.

Each of the six weeks of prayer focuses on one aspect of the cup as a metaphor of spiritual growth. It is my hope that this guide will both revitalize and enrich your relationship with the Divine. Take your time with each week—you may need a month to pray "a week"—it makes no difference. The most significant dimension of your journey with the cup is your intention of drawing near to God.

There is no perfect or best way to use this book. Much will depend on your own needs and individual spiritual path. I suggest the following for you, but please adapt it to a way that fits your own inner journey. It is vital that you pray in the way that is best for you. For instance, if you are a "night person," you might decide to pray late in the evening instead of in the recommended morning time. If attention to your breathing has not been a part of your spiritual practice, you may find that the suggested "Breathprayer" is more distracting than helpful for you.

Listen to the thoughts, desires, and feelings that arise within you. Trust that God is with you and will guide you. At times you will go beyond what I've suggested or you might change or skip some of the steps of the process. Do not doubt your own spiritual experience. You may have insights and feelings that are quite different from the ones that I have expressed. Trust the "Keeper of your cup" for guidance and direction.

A Time and a Place of Prayer

Choose a place and time where you will pray each day, preferably in the morning when you are still fresh and alert. If you live alone, finding a space may be relatively easy. If you live with even one other person, it may be difficult to find this space. Search for it. Find it. Claim it. Some solitude and quiet are essential in order to make this inner journey.

Your sacred space must fit your unique needs. I know someone who prays in the laundry room every day. Many find a corner in the bedroom. Some choose their office or their den. Wherever it might be, find the place and let it become your sacred spot. Choose a table, or even a small box or stool, on which to set your cup, a candle, and anything else that will speak of your spiritual journey. Have it there in front of you or beside your chair each day.

I hope that you will find at least twenty minutes a day to pray. It will mean making choices, setting priorities—perhaps less TV or fewer phone conversations or less newspaper reading or even fasting from one meal. On the other hand, this is not meant to induce guilt. On the days when you simply cannot complete, or maybe even begin, your prayer practice, let go and continue the next day.

Be aware of your feelings and where you let them take you. Some days you may be eager to enter into this process and other days you may wonder why you continue with it. Be sure to stay with the process especially on those days when you feel blah, restless, doubtful, stressed, or empty. This is often the time when the seeds of growth are germinating.

You are not alone if you find it frustrating and difficult to have the discipline, the desire, or the time for prayer. Our culture encourages busyness, not silence; activity, not quiet; extroversion, not introversion. Most of those who joined with me in praying with this book as a "trial run" struggled to be faithful to a daily quiet time. At the end of the six weeks, they all said that the struggle was well worth it. They noticed a change. It had deepened their awareness and their longing for God. It had created a desire in them to continue with a daily spiritual practice.

Meeting with Others

You may want to meet with a partner or a small group after each week is completed to both integrate and celebrate what has taken place during the week. There are suggested processes, rituals, and resources in the "Group Gatherings" chapter to facilitate the sharing and prayer of these gatherings.

Some "How To's" of Each
Day for Filling Your Cup of Life

1) Intention

Begin by reading the opening essay on the theme for the day. Then, make your "intention." The intention sets your inner direction. It will usually come from the theme for the day. This can be stated briefly in your own words such as: "I hope for this day to learn more about your love," or "I want to discover the clutter in my life," or "Teach me your ways," or "Help me to be compassionate." You might want to write this intention in your journal. Then, move to "The Daily Practice." ("Practice" means to do something frequently in order to make a habit of it or a way of life for yourself.)

2) Breathprayer

Each Daily Practice includes a "breathprayer." There is no set amount of time for the breathprayer. It can be prayed for as long as you wish. Many spiritual traditions have found that being attentive to our breathing is a helpful way to become centered or focused on our inner world. Breathing attentively, at an easy, regular pace, slows us down and calms our rushing mind and body. Sitting with the back straight is the recommended posture when doing breathprayer.

A word or brief phrase is suggested for you to say when you are breath-ing in and another word or phrase as you are breathing out. This is symbolic of the filling and emptying of the cup, the filling and emptying of our lives. (It also symbolizes birth, . . . the first in-breath, . . . and death, . . . the last out-breath of life.)

At first, this breathprayer may feel awkward and useless, but if you continue to do it each day, this practice can gradually become a helpful way to go within and to enter into your sacred time with God.

3) Reflection

You will always be asked to use your cup for this part of the Daily Practice. This is the time when you prayerfully make connections between your spiritual path and the cup. I suggest that you keep this cup on your "altar" throughout the six weeks and use it only for this time of prayer. Let it become your sacred vessel.

4) Scripture

Only a morsel (a verse or two) of scripture is offered so that you can savor its meaning and relish the message. This tiny selection from the Word of God is full of spiritual nutrition. The entire passage is also indicated in case you choose to read the verse in a larger context.

5) Journaling

You may not consider yourself to be a "writer," but please do gather the fruit of your reflection by writing, drawing, or painting in your journal each day, even if it is a very brief entry. There are questions and suggestions to get you started, but you may not need these. It makes no difference if your grammar or spelling is correct. You are the only one who will read what you have written.

The journal is a means of recording and preserving your experience so that you can go back and reflect upon it at another time. This is especially true if you are meeting with others at the end of each week. As you re-read your journal, you will be able to "gather up" the days. Another aspect of journal writing is that it tends to draw insights and feelings from us that may otherwise be missed. In the process of writing, we often come to greater consciousness, clarity, and perspective.

6) Connecting

In the "Today" section, a suggestion is given as a means of taking your prayer into the day with you. Do not be discouraged if you often forget about this suggestion as your day becomes filled with busyness. I encourage you, however, to make the effort of this integration as it can add a richness and a vitality to your daily relationships and to the tasks that are a part of your day.

7) Integrating

You will notice that Day 7 of each week is a "free day"—a "Sabbath" of sorts. This is the day for you to review the week, to ponder and integrate what has occurred, and to learn from the revelations of the past six days. Day 7 is a "be-ing" day of spiritual leisure and a celebration of all you have experienced during the past week of prayer. Enjoy!

Four Helpful "Signals"

Our "spiritual life" is not limited to a set time and place of prayer. Rather, it involves all of our life, every moment of our existence. God is always "happening" in our lives. We need to consistently nourish, restore, and renew this relationship. A regular practice of prayer is one way of doing this.

Through our daily practice, our inner antennae are re-alerted to discover God throughout our entire day. I believe that being faithful to a specific time of prayer each day can help us to wake up spiritually, to be more present to our relationships, to our work, and to whatever takes place in our lives. Just as some people wake up with a cup of coffee, so these reflection times can wake us up to how God is present in our every moment.

"Showing up," being faithful to our time of prayer, and being available to God, is essential. We need to "be there." I once guided a priest who had lost his enthusiasm and energy for prayer. During this difficult time he did not know how or what to pray, but he believed in being open and in "showing up" for his daily spiritual practice. This fidelity to openness and being present eventually transformed his spiritual journey. The same can be true for us.

Here are four quick reminders as you use this book:

Wake up: Be aware, open, ready to receive.

Show up: Discipline yourself to be there!

Shake up: Be willing to have your inner viewpoint rearranged.

Start up: Get moving. Take your relationship with God into your world. Let it make a difference in the way you live.

May you enter this process with a strong belief in the presence of God dwelling within you. May you continually renew your trust in God's wisdom and guidance as you make this journey.

The Evening Review

This brief review is meant to bring wholeness into your entire day, to wrap the day with the ribbon of prayer. Each evening, pause before you get into bed, or as you are undressing, or as you are lying in bed, and reflect upon the day you have just lived:

1. How open or aware was I to the presence of God in my day?

2. What kind of nourishment did I receive? What kind of nourishment did I give?

3. Does anything need to be emptied out in order for me to be at peace tonight?

4. For what do I thank God as I prepare to enter into sleep?

Close with this prayer or one of your own choice:

Divine Companion, shelter me under your wings of love. Grant me a peaceful night and a restful sleep. Amen.

Choosing a Cup

Before You Begin Week 1

Thoughtfully decide on a cup that you will use for your daily spiritual practice during the entire six weeks. Bless the cup with the following bless-ing prayer.

Blessing of the Cup

Bestower of Life, Abundant Love,
Trusted Companion, Eternal Wisdom,
I pray your blessing to be upon this cup and upon myself.
Make of this cup a sacred vessel
as I pray with it each day.
May this cup become my teacher,
helping me to find my way to you.
May this cup hold many messages
of your wisdom and your comfort.
May this cup connect me with life
and create in me a generous heart.
May this cup draw me ever closer
into loving oneness with you.

A Note About God-Language

How do we name the divine presence? With what images are we the most comfortable? I think that one of the most difficult aspects of inviting someone into prayer is "God language." The words that I use and find most meaningful in naming my perception and experience of God may be far different from what another person desires in addressing God. Some feel drawn to masculine metaphors such as "Father" or "Lord," and others may be more comfortable using feminine ones such as "Mother" or "Sophia." Others would prefer to address "Jesus" consistently, and still others would rather use more universal symbols such as "Higher Power."

Because of the great diversity of approaches in naming the Divine Being, I have most often simply used the word "God" when referring to this presence in the opening essays for each day. I have tried to use a variety of images in addressing the Divine Being in the Daily Practice. You are most welcome to substitute your own preferred naming of God in any of the places where my naming seems inadequate or uncomfortable for your spiritual path.

THE CUP OF LIFE

A View of the Week

Every time you listen with great attentiveness to the voice that calls you the Beloved, you will discover within yourself a desire to hear that voice longer and more deeply.

—Henri J. M. Nouwen

When I was a young child of eight years old, I lived on a beautiful farm. Like my other siblings, I had chores to do after school. Mine consisted of feeding the chickens and gathering the eggs. I didn't like doing this because my free spirit wanted to be out in the grove playing or down by the creek watching tadpoles and catching minnows.

But one day all of that changed for me. I learned that I had a secret companion who always kept me company, even when I was doing the daily farm chores. Hidden away deep within my heart was a loving being named God who would always love me and would never leave me. It was at this time that a wise teacher taught me about friendship with God. She assured me that I would never be alone because I was carrying the very life of God within me. I was enthused about this discovery. I could sense that "Someone" was there. I began carrying on endless conversations with this Friend. Walking home from school, doing my chores, playing in the grove—all of these activities became opportunities to be with my "special Someone." This was the beginning of my relationship with God.

As I grew older, I recognized this inner presence as a dynamic source of guidance and consolation. I became ever more deeply rooted in the belief that this indwelling God loves me totally and unconditionally. To this day, I draw comfort and courage from the belief that I am a container holding the presence of God. This awesome and humbling gift of the Divine Indwelling constantly enlivens my spiritual path and seeds my transformation.

The more I become aware of God's presence in my life, the more I thirst to know this Sacred One at an ever deeper and deeper level. Like a cup that seemingly has more and more room to be filled, so I feel that my capacity to be united with God keeps expanding. The more I know how loved I am by God (the more my cup is filled), the more I am always thirsting for more of God (seeing how much room the cup still has in it to receive).

When I think about the spiritual life, I think of a life with God that is healthy and vibrant. The root and foundation of this life is *relationship*. This relationship may have many struggles, crooked paths, and hidden corners, but at the core, there is a bond that is deep and strong. This relationship feeds and nourishes my inner self and gives a vitality and vibrancy to all of my life.

Each one of us is a temple of the Holy One. Each of us carries a spiritual power in us that can cause even the tiniest of faith-seeds to grow. It is vital that we protect and nurture this relationship so that it thrives. The cup of our spiritual life must be cared for and replenished as it pours its contents away in loving service. Like the cup with its boundaries, we, too, need parameters so that our life does not seep away into endless busy-ness and unguarded, unfocused activity.

This week I invite you to reflect on your relationship with God, to celebrate the beauty of this presence within you, to be grateful for the marvelous life flowing through your spirit. Be attentive to the One who dwells within you.

a simple container
has spoken
in my solitude,
a teacher
and bringer of wisdom

whispering truths
of an indwelling God
in the container
of my soul

hearkening to
my hidden ability
to be filled
and to pour
from a life
of abundance

reminding me
of necessary boundaries
for nurturing
the sacred space
within me

inviting me
to sip often from
the Divine wellspring,
source that slakes
my spiritual thirst

calling to me
like a seed
in the soil:

believe believe believe
in the power
that is present
in the life
that is possible

—Joyce Rupp

Day 1

The Cup of My Life

You are a love song
beauty set to music
You are a love song
I have chosen you.

—Theresa Hucal

It was a chilly evening in November when we gathered to mourn the death of my friend's beautiful Italian mother. The kinship of those who had loved her eased some of the heartache we were feeling. There was a special moment when the sadness in the room changed to a glow of love. I felt it as we listened to the singing of "You Are a Love Song." I sensed that each one of us was turning in memory to this woman and recalling how she had truly been a "love song" of God for the many people whose lives she had touched. She had been a cup of life for those who had known her. The things she had done with her life were not grandiose. They were simple, human endeavors. But out of those ordinary activities and experiences, she had brought many extraordinary songs of love to others.

What would it be like if we believed that we were a love song of God? How would it change our presence with others? While healthy spirituality requires a deep belief in our own loveableness, this belief is not always easy to accept. The cup can be a teacher in this. Think of the cup as a symbol of our unique self. Many coffee and tea cups have a special shape and size, a "personality," so to speak, just as each human person does. Like a cup, our physical, psychological, and spiritual shape is unique to each of us. We cannot take someone else's body, or spirituality, or personality and make it our own any more than a cup can change its color and shape to match each person who drinks from it. The cup is a good container no matter who uses it. It is of value in itself.

Too often people want someone else's spirituality rather than their own. I've discovered that the more I am conscious and accepting of God's love for me, the more I can accept myself and the unique way that my spiritual path unfolds. God created each of us out of love. We are beauty set to music. We are one-of-a-kind, unique, meant to be a light of love in transforming our world.

Even if you do not feel awe or gratitude or compassion when you think about yourself, try to believe it today. Ask God to help you to see yourself as a song of love, a cup full of goodness, bringing life to others.

THE DAILY PRACTICE

Breathprayer

> Breathing in: I am . . .
> Breathing out: . . . a love song

Reflection

> Hold the cup in your hands.
> Notice its style, shape, color, size.
> Be conscious of yourself as a cup held in God's hands.
> Accept your uniqueness and your goodness.
> Thank God for creating you as you are.

Scripture: Isaiah 43:1-7

> I have called you by name,
> You are mine. . . .
> You are precious in my sight,
> and honored, and I love you (Is 43:1,4).

Journaling (Choose one or more and respond.)

> When I think about God loving me unconditionally as I am, I . . .
>
> As I pray through these six weeks of spiritual guidance, I most desire . . .
>
> Dear God . . . (write a letter, a song, a psalm, a poem . . . to God).

I turn to you, Divine Creator, and I thank you for the person I am. I am a cup of life. I have love and goodness within me. Help me to hear your music in my soul today and to smile in gratitude when I think of my own uniqueness. Let me not doubt my value or question my worth. Help me to know and to accept who I am. I am yours. May I bring life to my world.

Today

I will try to be a love song for others this day.

Day 2

A Container of God's Presence

You are a dwelling place for the Source of all life.

—Macrina Wiederkehr

One of my favorite parts of the day is when I come in from my early morning walk and have a cup of freshly brewed, steaming hot coffee. On cold winter days, I especially like the feel of my favorite coffee mug in my hands and I thoroughly enjoy the sips of liquid that bring welcomed warmth into my body.

My coffee mug reminds me that cups are containers designed to hold something refreshing, just as we are containers meant to hold the Divine Presence. Because God dwells within me, I like to think of myself as a mini Ark of the Covenant. God goes with me wherever I go. I carry God into each relationship and experience. A powerful thought, that one.

Our understanding and our experience of God shapes our image of God and our spirituality. Who is God? Where do we find this God of ours? If we look at the Hebrew scriptures, we will find that the Divine Presence is everywhere, always moving and always calling to people, wherever they may be. If we look at the Christian scriptures, we find a significant addition: this Divine Presence has made a home *in us*. Jesus said, "Make your home in me" (Jn 15:4). He used the image of the vine and the branches to emphasize that the same life that surges through all parts of the plant is similar to the life of God that surges through our being. God is no longer just "out there." God is also here, within us. The spirit of Jesus lives on in our own bodily temples. We have become the home of God.

Some days I go zooming along, checking off all the "stuff" I have on my "to do" list, and I totally forget that I am the home of God. When this happens, I can easily lose my reverence and my awareness of all the beauty around me. On the other hand, when I remember that God has made a home in my heart and in the heart of each one I meet, I look at people and life quite differently. I am more patient and kind and much less judgmental.

As you move through this day, brush off the old dust and cobwebs caused by busyness and non-attention, and become aware of how God travels with you.

THE DAILY PRACTICE

Breathprayer

> Breathing in: Faithful Love . . .
> Breathing out: . . . dwelling in me

Reflection

> Hold your empty cup in your hands.
> Notice the space within the cup.
> Think of the space within yourself.
> It is filled with the Divine Presence.
> Draw near to this Loving Presence.
> Sense this Loving Presence permeating your entire being.
> Rest in silence and tranquility.
> Listen to God say to you: "I am here."

Scripture: John 15:1-11 or 1 Corinthians 3:1-17

Abide in me as I abide in you (Jn 15:4).

Do you not know that you are God's temple and that God's Spirit dwells in you? (1 Cor 3:16).

Journaling

I am most aware of God's dwelling within me when . . .

As I reflect on the Divine Presence dwelling within myself and others, I hope that . . .

Dear God . . .

Prayer

O Divine Presence, you have danced your way into my innermost being. O Mystery of Life, you have tended and nurtured me. You have enriched my spirit and watered my dryness. You have poured your abundant love into the veins of my soul. In the darkest of nights, you have surrounded me with your love. O Divine Presence, your radiant energy surges through my being. I bow to the profound mystery of your sacred life within me.

Today

Several times during the day I will quietly place my hand over my heart and remember with gratitude that God dwells within me.

Day 3

The Vessel of Loving Energy

The same stream of life
that runs through my veins
night and day
runs through the world
and dances in rhythmic measures.

—Rabindranath Tagore

I remember how I used to begin programs of spiritual growth. I would be intent on doing well. I would work very hard at it, often feeling concerned or anxious because I wanted to do it "right" and make a lot of progress. I felt like it all depended upon me as to whether or not I would grow. I did not yet realize that I needed the vibrant stream of divine life moving through me in order to be transformed.

This attitude gradually changed because of an experience I had on an eight-day retreat. I fell into a deep slump during that time and could not get myself to pray or connect with God. This complete loss of spiritual control allowed me to see painfully that my ego had been trying to control my inner journey. This experience taught me that I am simply an empty cup until I am filled with the loving energy of God. Once I became aware of this reality, I felt much more strength and serenity about my spiritual journey.

Personal growth does take some effort on my part. I do need to give myself to the process, but I cannot *force* growth to happen. This is God's realm of doing. I can yearn for transformation. I can be faithful to daily meditation. But as long as I am trying to go it alone, I will simply stumble along fruitlessly. Like the woman who touched the hem of Jesus' garment and received the healing power of his spirit, so I need to receive the life-changing energy of the divine love in my life (Lk 8:40-48).

One of the dangers of spiritual growth is that too much emphasis can be placed on "results," on how we are doing or how we are progressing. When we catch ourselves being anxious about the results of our prayer or wonder if we are changing fast enough, it is time to go back and ponder Ephesians 3:20.

This passage tells of God's power working through us and offers the assurance that this power is "able to accomplish abundantly far more than we can ask or imagine."

Today is a good day to remember that it is God who gives us the power to act and to change. It is good day to stop worrying about whether or not we are making progress.

THE DAILY PRACTICE

Breathprayer

> Breathing in: Your power . . .
> Breathing out: . . . moving through me

Reflection

> Hold the cup in your hands.
> Remember that the cup is a container.
> Set the cup down in front of you.
> Feel the pulse on your wrist or neck.
> Visualize the blood pumping through your body.
> See it sustaining your life, bringing you energy for growth.
> Close your eyes and sense God's goodness filling your spirit.
> Picture God's life pulsing through you.
> Welcome God's loving energy surging through your being.

Scripture: 2 Corinthians 4:5-12

> But we have this treasure in clay jars, so that it may be made clear that this extraordinary power belongs to God and does not come from us (2 Cor 4:7).

Journaling

> How have I known God's power working in me and through me?
> What are some obstacles blocking the flow of loving energy?
> What part of my life most needs the powerful touch of God?

___

Energizing and transforming God, the pulse of your presence fills my life with love. Remind me often that I cannot grow by my own efforts alone. Thank you for the comfort and the freedom of knowing that it is your power working through me that creates growth in my spiritual life.

Today

___

As I use any vessel today (a cup, a glass, a can of soda, etc.), I will remember that I am a vessel of God's tremendous loving energy.

___

Day 4

The Boundaries of the Cup

Energy is everywhere, but stillness plays a major role in its conversion from "potential" to "actualized" energy. At Callaway Gardens, I was amazed to learn that butterflies have to spread their wings in the morning sunshine because the scales on their wings are actually solar cells. Without that source of energy, they cannot fly.

—Laurie Beth Jones

"I'm falling apart." "I can't seem to get it together." "I just lost it." "This was a messy day." "I came unglued." When I make comments like that, I am usually feeling stressed, pressured, at odds with myself and maybe with others, too. Things don't "hang together" very well for me on days like that. When this happens I often have a feeling that all of my energy and time is draining away, that I am unable to contain it.

A similar sort of thing can happen on the spiritual path. Without some boundaries or discipline, it is difficult to establish and stay on a spiritual path that has depth and quality to it. I can feel lost, adrift, unable to find the time and space to pray and reflect as I would like. People, events, responsibilities, and multiple activities keep me hurrying and worrying with little time left for my inner self.

My cup speaks to me about boundaries. If the cup did not have the boundaries of sides and a bottom, it could not hold anything in it. The cup has an opening—it is able to give and receive—but the boundaries keep what it contains from being spilled everywhere. Likewise, we must have boundaries around the time we need to connect with our deeper selves. Otherwise, all sorts of situations, interferences, interruptions, and schedule pressures will cause this time to fall apart and be in great disarray. Everyone else cannot always come first. We need to value ourselves enough to spread our spiritual wings and receive God's energy. Even Jesus put himself first at those times when he prayed alone or went apart from his ministry so that he could renew his inner resources.

There are always exceptions. Sometimes we won't be able to pray when or where we choose, but many times it is simply a matter of setting some boundaries and being firm about keeping them. (Can we let the doorbell or phone ring without feeling compelled to answer? Can we let the stack of "undone things" go for a while?)

Take some time today to think about your spiritual boundaries. Are there any areas that need some attention?

THE DAILY PRACTICE

Breathprayer

> Breathing in: Guide me . . .
> Breathing out: . . . guard me

Reflection

> Hold your cup in your hands.
> Touch the sides and the bottom of the cup.
> Trace the outside of the cup with your fingers.

Run your fingers around the inside of the cup.
Close your eyes and imagine your spiritual boundaries.
Let yourself lean on God for a while.
Ask for whatever boundaries are needed in your spiritual life.
Listen to God speak to you about these boundaries.

Scripture: Matthew 14:22-27

And after he had dismissed the crowds, he went up the mountain by himself to pray. When evening came, he was there alone . . . . (Mt 14:22-23).

Journaling

What keeps me from having enough time to resource my inner life?

Here are some boundaries I will keep . . .

What might Jesus' prayer have been when he left his busy life to be alone?

Prayer

Help me to protect my relationship with you, God. Grant me the vision to see what may need to be changed and the courage to take a stand for my own time and space. May I value my spiritual life enough so that I will make good decisions in order to stay closely in touch with you. May my quiet time with you enrich and enhance the rest of my day so that I am able to find you in every part of it.

Today

I will make one decision regarding a boundary that will help protect my intentional time and place with God.

Day 5

The Cup as My Teacher

> The Celtic approach to God opens up a world in which nothing is too common to be exalted and nothing is so exalted that it cannot be made common.
>
> —Esther de Waal

So many books have been written about entering into a relationship with God. Some of these books make it seem like a giant undertaking when, actually, our life with God is so simple. Beginning where the Celtic tradition began, with the common and the ordinary, makes for a much healthier approach to spiritual growth. The cup is a teacher in this, for the cup is very ordinary and very much a part of the common events of the day. Like the spiritual gifts of my life, I often use my cup without ever considering its beauty or noticing how it serves my needs for refreshment.

I used to keep my spiritual life in a tight space and felt that my work, my social life, my relational joys and struggles actually kept me away from God rather than teaching me and being sources of personal transformation for me. Now I see all of this differently. I have come to believe that every part of my life affects or influences my life with God. The world I live in, with its beauty and tragedy, with its creatures of all forms and shapes, is constantly offering me messages about who I am and who God is. Everything and everyone teaches me about God, life, and myself.

I try now to approach each person, event, creature, with two questions: How are you my teacher? What am I meant to learn?

God is dwelling with us everywhere. For our part we need to have awareness or consciousness of this loving presence. Our meditation and prayer time can be a source of our waking up, becoming more aware of God always filling our days and nights. The most ordinary of our days contains the power and the splendor of spiritual awareness. It is up to us to pay attention, to be present to the here and now, in order to enter more deeply into life.

As we open ourselves to spiritual growth, there is simply no part of our life that can be left out. Nothing is too dirty or smudged. Nothing is too ecstatic or passionate. Nothing is too mundane or ordinary. *All* of life is the food of our spiritual growth. We can grow closer and deeper in our relationship with God through every situation, depending on our attitude, our openness, and our awareness. Be aware of God teaching you through your life today.

THE DAILY PRACTICE

Breathprayer

> Breathing in: O Mystery . . .
> Breathing out: . . . alive in me!

Reflection

> Hold your cup in your hands.
> Look closely at it.
> What does the cup teach you today?
> Turn inwardly to God.
> Listen.
> Ask God to keep you attentive today.

Scripture: Luke 12:22-31 (how Jesus learned from life)

> Consider the ravens: they neither sow nor reap . . . yet God feeds them. . . . Consider the lilies, how they grow: they neither toil nor spin, yet even Solomon in all his glory was not clothed as one of these (Lk 12:24, 27).

Journaling

> When I think of the cup as my teacher, I . . .
> One way in which life has been my teacher is . . .
> Today I long to learn . . .

Prayer

> Creator and Sustainer of Life, all of life is my teacher! May I see, hear, touch, taste, feel, with greater awareness. May I relate to

others in a more meaningful way. May I not brush aside any part of my day without being attentive to the truth that it holds for me. O Mystery of Life, be my guide today. Amen.

Today

I will notice something very ordinary today and learn from it.

Day 6

Thirsting for Filling

As truly as there is in God a property of compassion . . . so truly there is in God a property of thirst and longing. By virtue of this longing in Christ, we have to long for God in response. . . . The property of longing thirst comes from the endless goodness of God. . . . Spiritual thirst will last in God as long as we are in need, drawing us up to God's bliss.

—Julian of Norwich

It is a rare day when we are completely satisfied. Usually we are hoping, wishing, longing, thirsting for something more, something different, something else we think will satisfy us or make our lives happier. We are often like an empty cup waiting to be filled with whatever it is we think is missing in our lives.

There are many kinds of inner thirsting. Not to thirst for things of the ego such as recognition, prestige, power, and success is very difficult. Once we shake ourselves loose from these longings, our spirit will be freer to thirst for the deeper things of God. We will be much more intent on asking for the living water for our thirsty soul instead of the things that feed our thirsty ego.

What are some of the thirsts of a deeper nature? What are the longings that arise from the core of our being? What are the yearnings of our heart in relation to our God? Some of these deeper thirsts or longings might be:

- peace of mind and heart
- healing of old wounds
- greater acceptance of ourselves
- justice for anyone who is exploited
- discovery of who we truly are
- harmony with our families and our workplace
- wisdom to make good choices and decisions
- forgiveness of ourselves and others
- freedom from false messages of our mind
- reverence and enthusiasm for life
- a willingness to hear God's voice

Let us look deeply into our lives today to see the nature, the quality, and the intensity of our thirsts. Let us ask God for living water for our soul and then hold our waiting cup to receive.

THE DAILY PRACTICE

Breathprayer

> Breathing in: Thirsting, thirsting . . .
> Breathing out: . . . for you, God

Reflection

> Hold the empty cup in your hands.
> Let the emptiness remind you of your yearnings.
> For whom and what do you most yearn or thirst?
> Now hold the cup close to your heart.
> Be thirsty for God.
> Be filled with God.

Scripture: Psalm 63

> O God, you are my God,
> I seek you,
> my soul thirsts for you;
> my flesh faints for you,
> as in a dry and weary land
> where there is no water (Ps 63:1).

Journaling

> I thirst for . . .
> My spiritual thirst has been quenched when . . .
> O God . . .

Prayer

> God, of your goodness give me yourself, for you are enough for me.
> I can ask for nothing less that is completely to your honor, and if
> I do ask for anything less, I shall always be in want. Only in you I
> have all. (Julian of Norwich)

Today

> I will deliberately let myself be physically thirsty. I will let my thirst
> remind me of my inner thirst for God.

Day 7

Integration/Review

1. Visit and review your past six days.

2. Highlight anything in your journal that particularly touches you with its truth.

3. Write a brief summary of this week. (Alternatives for this summary would be to use paints, clay, dance . . . or you could draw a cup and let the size, shape, form, contents, and message on it symbolize what you experienced this week.)

Memo

Are you remembering to spend a few minutes each evening in a review of your day? Have you looked each night before you go to sleep to see how empty or how full your day has been? Have you noticed the gifts that are a part of each day?

If you've forgotten about doing this, refer to the "Introduction" chapter in which this "evening review" is described.

THE OPEN CUP

Day 1: The Cluttered Cup
Day 2: Space for Listening
Day 3: The Empty Cup
Day 4: Readiness to Receive
Day 5: Trusting
Day 6: Solitude
Day 7: Integration/Review

A View of the Week

If the doors of my heart ever close,
I am as good as dead.

—Mary Oliver

Every once in a while I have a moment of sheer panic. One of these moments occurred the night I came home late from a meeting and discovered that my screen door had been accidentally locked. I immediately looked to see if there was any other way into the house. There were no openings. After much consternation, I finally discovered that I could pry open the screen door and pop the lock. What a relief to open up the door to my home that evening.

Almost everything needs to be opened to serve its purpose. Clothes need to be opened before we can put them on to receive their warmth and protection. A book requires opening before the contents can be shared. A house has to have a door or window opened before it can provide us shelter. A cupboard door must be opened before the contents can be retrieved.

The same holds true for our spiritual self. Being open is a prerequisite for spiritual growth. For God to enter our lives fully, we must be ready to receive. The door to our inner self must be wide open. Our mind and heart need to be receptive so that we can hear and receive what God is offering us. God needs openings in our lives to "get through to us," to communicate with us, to nourish us, to stretch us toward greater growth, to revitalize and renew us with love.

Openness is also about wonder and surprise. Christin Lore Weber writes: "All life is a beginning. I need an open, spontaneous, joyful attitude that knows it does not know. I need an emptiness in me. . . . I need to find the part in my soul still empty, still able to be surprised, still open to won-der" (*The Finding Stone*). Oftentimes a deep joy is associated with openness because openness leads to inner freedom and growth.

This freedom usually comes with a price. It requires trusting God more with our lives and having a willingness to meet our resistances head-on. I never like facing what keeps me from being open, but as long as I thrash around in my wild attempts to clutch and cling to old securities, I close myself off from the growth that could be mine.

Sometimes we may be open but not have much room to receive, due to the inner clutter that junks up and crowds our mind and heart. This clutter claims a lot of mental and emotional space and keeps us from receiving the good things we need. Just as our bodies breathe in oxygen and breathe out carbon dioxide, so our spirits need to take in what is life-giving and empty out what is not helpful for us.

This week I invite you to ponder your openness and to take some brave steps to empty out anything that might be keeping your spiritual cup from being filled. I also invite you to remain faithful to your time of solitude, the time in which you pay full attention to your relationship with God. The daily practice of solitude prepares and nurtures your readiness to receive from God throughout your day. Solitude can help you to refocus your intentions, to listen more fully, and to clear away some of the inner debris that obstructs your spiritual openness.

As you pray through this week, may you continue to open the space within yourself that is waiting to be filled with the radiance of God.

Generous God
so many times I've come
with my empty cup
a beggar of the heart
devoid of nourishment
depleted of energy

and you have filled

Generous God
so many times I've come
afraid of unknowns
full of negatives and no's
fighting the challenges
closed and resistant to
growth

and you have opened

Generous God
so many times I've come
a stranger to my spirit
crammed with cultural noise
caught in endless clutter
crowding my inner space

and you have emptied

Generous God
I come to you again
holding out my waiting cup
begging that it first be emptied

of all that blocks the way
then asking for its filling
with love that tastes like you

—**Joyce Rupp**

Day 1

The Cluttered Cup

Our minds are like crows. They pick up everything that glitters, no matter how uncomfortable our nests get with all that metal in them.

—Thomas Merton

I don't know about you, but it seems like I am forever trying to get rid of the physical clutter in my life. I just get my heaping basket of correspondence emptied, and it's full again. I finally clear off the top of my desk, and the next week it's messier than it ever was. I dust the house and put things away only to have to re-do it again soon afterward. It seems like there is always a stack of something waiting to be sorted and discarded.

The same is true for me spiritually. There are so many kinds of inner clutter. Things like anxiety, resentment, harsh judgments, self-pity, and mistrust can take up a lot of inner space. The strident voices, negative thoughts, useless fears and worries, old wounding messages, and the "have to's and want to's" that bully me around, squeeze out the good things that are waiting for me.

One sunny March morning as I was taking my usual walk up a high hill near my home, I noticed all sorts of trash and discarded items on the grass along the sidewalk. The discarded debris on that one short block was unbelievable. It pained me to look at it. The next day when I trudged by that same trash I was in a foul mood, doing a lot of grumbling inside of myself. Suddenly I saw that I was a lot like that uphill walk. I had a long trail of clutter and debris inside of me. My negativity was cluttering my spirit, keeping me from receiving the joy of the day.

Anything can be clutter if it keeps me totally absorbed in myself and unaware of what God is offering to me. Even very wonderful things such as success, knowledge, beauty, and pleasure can become "clutter" when I seek these things madly and at any cost, obsessed with having more, clutching them closely to me, or putting all my energy into preserving them. I do not have to discard these good things, but I do need to keep them from taking over my inner life. Clutter throws me off-balance when I let it take over my mind or my emotions. There is not much room for God's agenda when mine takes up all the nooks and crannies. Even prayer itself can become clutter if my spiritual practice becomes the focal point instead of my relationship with God.

Today be patient with yourself as you evaluate your clutter and decide what needs to go. It takes time to sort through and discard what one has collected over a lifetime!

THE DAILY PRACTICE

Breathprayer

> Breathing in: Let go . . .
> Breathing out: . . . unclutter

Reflection

> Sit quietly. Go within.
> Look around inside.
> See what clutters your life with God.
> Then take your cup.
> Imagine or picture this clutter being in your cup.
> Lift the cup and turn it sideways.
> Symbolically empty out the clutter of your inner life.
> Now turn the cup back up and sit quietly.
> Let the freedom of non-clutter pervade your spirit.
> Try to feel the joy of a non-cluttered heart.

Scripture: Matthew 6:19-21

> For where your treasure is, there your heart will be also (Mt 6:21).

Journaling

> Write a dialogue with God about your inner clutter.
> Make a list of the clutter in your life.

The inner clutter that is most difficult to discard is . . . because . . .

Shine the light of your love on my spirit, God.
Help me to see what gets in the way.
Grant me the strength to empty out my clutter.
Thank you for your power working through me.
May I walk into this day with a deeper awareness of our union.

Today

Put your cup on its side and place the list halfway in and halfway out of the cup, as a sign of your desire to empty your life of unnecessary clutter. Try to discard one piece of clutter today.

Day 2

Space for Listening

When we pray, how often do we say: "Speak, Lord, for your servant is listening"? More often, I think, we say: "Listen, Lord, for your servant is speaking!"

—Robert Wicks

I have a friend who periodically loses her voice and has to speak in whispers. One day she called me and whispered for fifteen minutes. It took a lot of energy for me to listen intently so that I could hear what she had to say. I think this is what it is like to be attentive to God. God often speaks in whispers. If my life is crowded and cluttered with many thoughts and feelings pushing their way around inside of my head and heart, I may easily miss hearing what it is that God wants me to hear.

Listening attentively is essential for spiritual growth. To do this, we need open minds and hearts, emptied of the clutter that blocks our way and crowds out what awaits entrance into our life. Listening is especially difficult to do because our external world is so full of noise. We are constantly bombarded with the noise of traffic, television, and numerous machines that tend to run our lives for us. We unconsciously learn how to tune out or ignore many of these noises when we are not deliberately paying attention to them. As we become accustomed to tuning out these external things, we develop a pattern of not listening internally as well.

Besides clearing out some of the noise and the ceaseless activity, I think that listening also requires that we become more comfortable with "be-ing." "Be-ing" helps us to develop awareness, to focus more keenly on our inner activity without needing to do anything except be attentive. Beatrice Bruteau writes: "Listening is a non-productive, contemplative activity, a kind of striving not to strive, for self-striving would make noise and prevent us from hearing . . ." (*Radical Optimism*). This is tough to do, especially if we live in a culture that promotes constant activity and productivity.

Every part of our life has something to offer us for our growth because God is there in the midst of it. When I give myself to attentiveness and deep listening, I find that I discover God everywhere. I "hear" connections with my deeper life in music, in correspondence I receive, in telephone calls, in the people I meet, in what I read and touch and taste, and in the insights and emotions that arise within me.

Listen. . . . What do you hear?

THE DAILY PRACTICE

Breathprayer

> Breathing in: I listen . . .
> Breathing out: . . . You are here

Reflection

> Hold the cup in your open hands.
> See how the cup sits there quietly.
> Picture yourself in the Divine One's hands.
> Go to the stillness deep within yourself.
> Allow yourself to be attentive.
> Just "be" with God.
> Listen.

Scripture: Psalm 85:8-13

> Let me hear what God will speak,
> for God will speak peace to the people . . .
> to those who turn to God in their hearts (Ps 85:8).

Journaling

> Dear God, what do you want me to know about "be-ing?" What keeps me from listening to the voice of the Holy One? I have connected with my inner world recently when . . .

Prayer

> O God, you constantly try to get my attention. You stir and call in the most unlikely places of my life—people and situations that

I dismiss as not being able to contain your presence. You beckon me to those corners of my inner being where I've yet to discover you. Open me so that I will not miss your presence today. Help me to learn how to "be" and to let go of my need to be swallowed in activity.

<u>Today</u>

For one hour today I will be especially attentive to every piece of my life so that I will find God there.

Day 3

The Empty Cup

A door opens in the center of our being and we seem to fall through it into immense depths which, although they are infinite, are all accessible to us; all eternity seems to have become ours in this one placid and breathless contact. God touches us with a touch that is emptiness and empties us.

—**Thomas Merton**

There's a part of me that always wants to be filled, to feel good, to have life go well, and to not have any pain or discomfort. Yet, I know that a cup that is always full does not have room to receive. It does not have space to contain anything more than what it already has. Likewise, a cup that is never used or shared will grow stale and tasteless.

The spiritual path is a constant cycle of emptying and filling, of dying and rising, of accepting and letting go. The full cup is repeatedly emptied so that it can be filled again and again. This emptying happens in many ways. Sometimes I choose to be emptied of my fullness when I get involved in a situation where someone's life asks for a lot of my time and energy. This emptying can be draining, but it might also be rewarding and satisfying because I have a sense of truly giving to another.

At other times, life empties my cup without ever asking my permission. Challenging, inconvenient, messy, struggling, frustrating experiences constantly empty me. I am also emptied when I choose to let go of my habits and behaviors that are harmful to myself and to others.

While the process of emptying may be painful, it can also be "growthful." The empty times may feel useless, fruitless, and non-productive, but they are actually a means of our falling into the immense depths within ourselves where we see more clearly, learn to be less controlling, long more deeply for God, and touch life with greater reverence and gratitude. We enter into the deep realm inside of us that is filled with the mystery, awe, and endless beauty of God. Emptiness is a gift that opens us further to the transforming power of God.

Fasting from food or liquids is a way to physically deprive ourselves (to empty ourselves) of some of our fullness. It is one way of reminding ourselves of the need to be emptied from time to time. Bodily fasting can strengthen us for other kinds of emptying.

This might be a day when you will choose to physically fast so that you can gain courage in letting your full cup be emptied when it is time to do so.

THE DAILY PRACTICE

Breathprayer

(Be especially aware of the emptying-filling cycle as you breathe in and out.)

Breathing in: Filling up . . .
Breathing out: . . . emptying out

Reflection

Look into your empty cup.
Hold the empty cup between your hands.
Look into the emptiness.
Abide with the emptiness.

Do not attempt to fill it with insights or feelings.
Open the door of your heart.
Go inside and be with God.

Scripture: Philippians 2:1-11

Let the same mind be in you that was in Christ Jesus, who, though he was in the form of God, did not regard equality with God as something to be exploited, but emptied himself . . . (Phil 2:5-6).

Journaling

When I hear the word "emptiness" I feel . . .
When it comes to being empty, my experience has been . . .
Jesus, Emptied One . . .

Prayer

Jesus, you know what it is like to be totally emptied. Teach me the value of emptiness. Help me to not be frightened when my full cup is poured out. Come with your strength, your peace, your hope. Stand with me in my emptying times so that I will remain open and ready to grow.

Today

I will fast (deliberately deprive myself of something such as food, drink, certain thoughts, reading, or watching television) to remind myself of the need to "empty out."

Day 4

Readiness to Receive

Clay is molded into vessels, and because of the space where
there is nothing, you can carry water. Space is carved out from
a wall, and because of the place where there is nothing, you can
receive light. Be empty, and you will remain full. . . .

—Lao-Tsu

I was in the midst of facilitating a discussion on emptiness when one of the
conference participants spoke. She described the great sorrow and the long
siege of depression that she had just been through. Then she said to us, "I
think that the greatest gift of my emptiness was that I could not give. All I
could do was receive."

How much easier it is for most of us to give than it is to receive. When
we are in a giving mode, we are generally strong and in charge. Sometimes
we have to be brought to our knees before we are ready to receive. This is
when events and circumstances of life take over and do the emptying for
us. Maybe a bout of extended illness, or the trauma of a divorce, or the
heartache of a loved one's death empties us. When we cannot stand on our
own strength, when we do not have the inner resources we normally have,
we are being readied to receive. When we are empty and poor inside, we
finally realize that we have to rely on someone else giving us what we need.

Many things are given to us when we are receptive—gifts such as a
deeper understanding about ourselves and about life, a stronger union with
God, a much fuller appreciation of friends and loved ones, a new look at
things we so easily took for granted, a renewed vision of life that we only
dimly glimpsed before.

At first we may not be receptive to what is being offered. What is being
poured into the receptive cup of our hearts may seem to be unneeded by us,
or it may initially challenge us, or frighten us. We may not want to hear the
truth about our illusions, or to take a giant risk of change, or to make a huge

leap of belief in ourselves and others, or to accept a love like God's that is so total and unconditional.

Eventually we learn how wonderful it is to receive and we become more open and receptive. We receive more graciously, accepting the gifts that we need for our growth. We become more confident because we learn that at the heart of all the gifts is the treasure of Divine Love, poured out profusely into our open, emptied, readied hearts.

THE DAILY PRACTICE

Breathprayer

> Breathing in: I am ready . . .
> Breathing out: . . . I receive

Reflection

> Hold the empty cup in your hands.
> Look at all the room the cup has for filling.
> Picture the inner part of yourself.
> Notice how much room there is for filling.
> Hold the cup out before you in the gesture of a beggar.
> Ask God to fill you.
> Arise, go and slowly pour something in your cup (coffee, tea, water).
> Come back and sit down.
> Receive and enjoy the contents of the cup.

Scripture: Psalm 81

> Open your mouth wide and I will fill it. . . .
> I would feed you with the finest of wheat
> and with honey from the rock
> I would satisfy you (Ps 81:10,16).

Journaling

> Reflect on a time in your life when you felt very empty and received

something you needed for your life. Describe this experience.
What do I find most difficult about receiving?
What would help me to be more ready to receive graciously?

Prayer

Gracious Giver, you have so much that you want to share with me. Help me to recognize and let go of my fears, misgivings, doubts, and apprehensions. Remove any obstacles that keep me from being ready to receive what you desire for me. May I be receptive to the outpouring of your love and your wisdom.

Today

When others offer me help in any form, I will receive it graciously and with gratitude.

Day 5

Trusting

If you trust absolutely, you will always be receptive enough to the signals that life and God and yourself—your deep self— will be giving you. You will always be given the clue, the information, and the inspiration to carry you through.

—Andrew Harvey

Emptying asks that we have a willingness to grow. It also asks that we trust God with our lives, that we believe God is for us and not against us, that we trust God not to abandon us in our time of need. Trust is the foundation of love.

St. Teresa of Avila prayed that she would let God be enough for her. There are many times when I find this notion extremely challenging. When I have times of emptiness, I sometimes ask God: "Are you enough for me? Can I be satisfied with just having you and not having whomever or whatever is being emptied out of my life?" I *do* want God to be enough for me so that I do not go seeking for things to take the place of this Loving Presence in my life, but it is easy to waver and to doubt that "God is enough" in my moments of insecurity or pain. It's a crazy thing, but as much as I find myself longing for God, it is sometimes excruciating to have nothing but God.

I learned a lot about my need to trust God some years ago when I was lying on my back, waiting to be wheeled into the surgery room. There were many unknowns about what the operation would reveal, and I had been very anxious about the situation. I wanted to be filled with answers instead of empty questions. As I lay there wishing that I was any place but in a hospital, words of surrender formed in my spirit. I was able to truly pray: "Into your hands, I surrender my life." As I did this, a most profound peace came over me. In that graced moment, I completely placed my trust in God and let God be enough for me. I knew then that whatever happened, it would be all right because God was with me.

Trusting God with our lives can be difficult because we often feel vulnerable when emptying happens. Yet the more we are at home with God, the more we can let go of our fears. Today is a good day to think about "trust." Think about your history of trust with human beings. The more trust we experience in our human relationships, the more likely it is that we will be open and free in our trust of God. If your trust has been wounded by others, ask God to restore your confidence. Let God be enough for you today.

THE DAILY PRACTICE

Breathprayer

> Breathing in: I trust you . . .
> Breathing out: . . . with my life

Reflection

> Place your cup in a safe spot in front of you.

Let it remind you of your desire to receive God's love.
Close your eyes.
Draw near to God.
Allow yourself to feel safe there.
Enjoy this secure haven.
Let God be enough for you.
Embrace God's love as you are enfolded in peace.

Scripture: Psalm 56

When I am afraid, I put my trust in you.
This I know, that God is for me (Ps 56:2,9).

Journaling

What keeps me from trusting God with my life?
I remember people whom I have trusted and who held that trust in a safe haven for me. (List these names. Recall what it was about them that gave you a sense of safety and trust.)
Write a dialogue with God. Ask God about trust and about "being enough" for you.

Prayer (based on the prayer of St. Teresa of Avila)

Let nothing disturb me, nothing frighten me. Let nothing take away my peace. May I wait with trust, with patience, knowing you will provide for me. I lack for nothing in you, God. You are my strong foundation. You are enough for me.

Today

When something or someone challenges my inner peace, I will turn to God, trusting that I will be given guidance and strength.

Day 6

Solitude

I lose my center. I feel dispersed, scattered, in pieces. I must have time alone in which to mull over any encounter, and to extract its juice, its essence, to understand what has really happened to me as a consequence of it.

—May Sarton

As we empty the cup of ourselves, we have more space in our life for what is truly of value. This space frees us to receive the truths that arise from our deeper selves when we slow down and quiet the rush of our life. Solitude helps us to listen, to see with greater inner clarity what needs to be emptied and what needs to be received. Solitude refreshes our awareness of God and of ourselves.

Solitude is the empty space that we deliberately choose in order to be with the Beloved. In solitude we can savor this goodness and give ourselves space to really listen. When we are occupied with life's many details and are rushing about in the marketplace, only the surface things of life usually get our attention. Solitude can help us to disengage and detach. It is when we are alone, uninterrupted, single-minded, and single-hearted, that some of the wonderful inner fruits come to the surface. If we want to learn how to grow spiritually, we will need the discipline of solitude.

Solitude is not always comfortable and comforting. It is not meant to always be a contented experience. Sometimes we come face to face with parts of ourselves that we have tried to avoid or ignore because they hurt too much or they challenge us too greatly.

Solitude can be a lonely, restless time, or a time when painful memories visit us. When we experience restlessness, loneliness, or other unwanted emotions in our solitude, we stay there with them. We don't run away. We sit with our tears or our joy. We let our hunger for God growl in our hearts. We listen to the pain. We have compassion for ourselves. We trust that whatever is in our solitude will eventually bear fruit because God is there with us.

As we mature on the spiritual path, all the moods and modes of our solitude are simply accepted as they are. We do less grasping of what we want and less pushing away of what we do not want. Our solitude helps us to "be" with God. It gives meaning to our lives. It reawakens us to the presence of God in every aspect of our lives.

Give yourself to solitude. God awaits you there.

THE DAILY PRACTICE

Breathprayer

> Breathing in: God . . .
> Breathing out: . . . my Beloved

Reflection

> Set your cup alone on a spot near you.
> Clear away everything else.
> Let this solitary cup call you to your own solitude.
> Let go of what you expect to happen during this time.
> Relax and repeat slowly: "God, you are enough for me."
> Smile as you repeat this wonderful truth.
> Allow the message to be deep within you.

Scripture: Matthew 6:5-6

> But whenever you pray, go into your room and shut the door and pray to your God who is in secret (Mt 6:4).

Journaling

> My struggles with solitude are . . .
> My blessings of solitude are . . .
> God, my Beloved . . .

Prayer

> Beloved of my soul, I long to embrace you.
> I savor the love that you offer to me.

I accept the challenges.
I receive the truths meant to transform me.
Grant me the courage to not run away.
I let go of my expectations and timetable.
May this solitude influence the totality of my life.

I will carry my solitude time into the rest of my day. I will receive each part of the day from God.

Day 7

Integration/Review

1. Visit and review your past six days.

2. Highlight anything in your journal that particularly touches you with its truth.

3. Write a brief summary of this week. (Alternatives for this summary would be to use paints, clay, dance, or you could draw a cup and let the size, shape, form, contents, and message on it symbolize what you experienced this week.)

Memo

How are you experiencing the practice of breathprayer? Is it helpful? Difficult? Distracting? Seemingly meaningless?

If being attentive to breathing in and out gets in your way and you lose your focus, just concentrate on the words for the in-breath and the out-breath. Let the breathing take care of itself. If it is the words that are getting in your way, concentrate on your breathing in and out and forget about the words.

Relax. Keep your back straight. Trust God to teach you.

THE CHIPPED CUP

A View of the Week

The Sufis say that real truth is always spoken with love. . . . Can we approach ourselves with kindness, may we be loving and gentle with ourselves, with our clumsiness, with our slowness to change, with our habits, with our tender hearts?

—Wayne Muller

One day my friend Pat told me about a bowl that her mother had given her long ago. She described it as having a lovely oriental design on it, used often for family gatherings over many years. She said that gradually the design faded and one side received a crack and several chips on it from so much use. Pat told me how she used to turn the "bad side" of the bowl to the wall of the china closet so that the flaws would be less noticeable. Now, however, she turns the bowl's faded, chipped area to the outside of the room so all can see and enjoy the stories it has to tell. Pat explained that as she aged she began to identify with the bowl, seeing her life reflected in it. She said, "It's like me. I've got some definite character marks from life, too."

We both laughed as I looked at her lovely aging face and thought of all she had experienced. It's true—life marks us both externally and interiorly if we really live it. The "perfect bowls" are the ones that oftentimes are never used to bring joy to others because they are carefully kept behind glass doors or hidden in cupboards collecting dust. They never really get to engage in life or enjoy nurturing others.

Flaws and inadequacies come with the territory of being human. Like Pat's bowl, or one of our well-used coffee or tea cups, we also have our bumps, scratches, cracks, and chips that keep us from being completely perfect vessels of life. We have our physical imperfections (whatever is inadequate by our culture's standards), and we have our internal inadequacies or stains of the spirit. Many people long to develop qualities they admire in others and struggle with not being capable enough in some facet of their life.

I used to think, "If I can just get rid of these things that I don't like about myself, then life will run smoothly. I'll feel a lot better about myself. Others will like me more." While there is a certain truth in some of this, there is also an underlying falseness: no matter how "good" I am, life will not always run smoothly, and I will always have some flaws. I won't always feel wonderful and certainly not all people are going to like me no matter how "perfect" I am.

I now think differently about my flaws. I see how being fully human is a paradox. Growing and becoming more of a person whose life resembles the values of Jesus is essential. At the same time, my flaws are some of my greatest treasures, like grains of sand in oyster shells that must grate and irritate to become pearls. My imperfections keep my ego in check. They remind me daily of how much I need the grace of God. They help me to be more understanding and compassionate with the inadequacies of others. They also give me the opportunity to continue to grow and change. Many times my inadequacies are what give the real flavor to my life.

At the same time, accepting myself doesn't mean I can excuse my behavior and actions that deliberately bring harm to myself or to others. I need to be cleansed of these stains. If the cup is never washed, eventually it will be full of grime. I must "come clean" like the cup and let my beauty shine.

Accepting our less-than-perfect selves is one of those big hurdles that we need to face to mature on the spiritual path. While it is essential for us to continually grow into more loving persons, it is equally important for us to value and accept who we are. This is a week not to criticize ourselves because of our flaws but, rather, to look at them and see what they can tell us about our relationships with God and with others.

it is time for me
to see the flaws
of myself
and stop
being alarmed

it is time for me
to halt my drive
for perfection
and to accept
my blemishes

it is time for me
to receive
slowly evolving growth
the kind that comes
in God's own good time
and pays no heed
to my panicky pushing

it is time for me
to embrace
my humanness
to love
my incompleteness

it is time for me
to cherish
the unwanted
to welcome
the unknown
to treasure
the unfulfilled

if I wait to be
perfect
before I love myself
I will always be
unsatisfied
and ungrateful

if I wait until
all the flaws, chips,
and cracks disappear
I will be the cup
that stands on the shelf
and is never used

—Joyce Rupp

Day 1

The Perfect Cup

Perfectionism is the voice of the oppressor, the enemy of the people. It will keep you cramped and insane your whole life.

—Anne Lamott

I was guiding the retreat of a clergyman, and the days were powerful for him. He had slowly come to terms with who he was: a person full of strengths and weaknesses who was deeply loved by God. As our time together came to a close, I decided to give him a cup as a reminder of the emptying and filling days of his retreat.

At the gift shop a large white cup with many red hearts on it caught my eye. As I picked it up, I noticed that the handle had a chip on it. I immediately thought, "Oh, too bad—this would have been just right for him." I set the cup down, but then I suddenly realized that this was exactly the right one for him. He had finally begun to let go of his belief that he had to be perfect before God could love him. The beautiful cup with the chip could daily remind him of this new realization.

Scripture scholars point out that the verse, "Be perfect as your heavenly Father is perfect," has been translated inaccurately. The actual text reads: "Be whole as God is whole." Wholeness implies a process, a gradual coming together into a oneness in which all the parts are integrated, but not necessarily perfect. Wholeness or holiness takes a lifetime of ups and downs. It can never be accomplished apart from divine help and guidance or without the interaction of our lives with others.

When we put most of our focus on our faults and our flaws, we tend to give most of our energy to this. Louise Hay comments: "We need to stop criticizing ourselves because criticism doesn't help—it just keeps us stuck in our problems" (*You Can Heal Your Life*). When we get sucked into constant self-criticism, we lose our perspective and forget our goodness. We also lose sight of the fact that it is God who helps us to grow. When the goal is "to be perfect" we can thrash around in our flaws and forget about loving others and sharing our gifts with them. We allow the desire to be perfect to oppress us and keep us in the bondage of self-preoccupation. The focus becomes "me" and the effort becomes "trying to perform perfectly."

Notice what you accept and what you reject about yourself and others. Be aware of your expectations. How much does "being perfect" influence your attitude and actions?

THE DAILY PRACTICE

Breathprayer

Breathing in: Loved, loved . . .
Breathing out: . . . loved as I am

Reflection

Hold your cup in your hands.
Study the cup.
Notice if there are any flaws or imperfections.
Enjoy the cup for itself: color, shape, size, etc.
Close your eyes. Picture yourself in God's hands.
See God observing how you look on the inside and outside.
Let God see your blemishes and faults.
Imagine God smiling and enjoying who you are.

Scripture: Psalm 139

For it was you who formed my inward parts;
you knit me together in my mother's womb.
I praise you for I am . . . wonderfully made.
Wonderful are your works (Ps 139:13-14).

Journaling

Make a list of your expectations of a) yourself and b) others.
Write a dialogue between God and the part of yourself that you especially struggle with accepting.
Dear God, when I picture you smiling and enjoying who I am, I . . .

Dear God, a long time ago I learned that you never make junk. You created me as a human person whose journey of life is the path to wholeness. This journey needs room for growth and space for evolving discovery. Each day is another opportunity to receive your help and your love as I become the person I am meant to be. Help me to love myself well and to entrust my growth to your guidance.

Remind me often that I am "wonderfully made" (Ps 139:14).

Today

I will not criticize or find fault with myself or others.

Day 2

The Shadow of the Cup

Making friends with your shadow helps facilitate your acceptance of yourself as a less-than-perfect human being. We have a dark side; we are not all light.

—**William A. Miller**

Whatever stands in the light casts a shadow. We've probably all heard various versions of the story about a person who wants to escape his or her shadow and cannot outrun it. There is obviously a parallel with our inner life. We, too, discover parts of our personalities that we do not want and that we hope we can outrun or escape in some way.

Well-known Swiss psychiatrist C. G. Jung described the "shadow" as anything in our inner world that we do not know or that we know but refuse to accept. It is the part of our psyche, or self, that is in the dark. The shadow can be a positive quality. It might be self-esteem in a woman who has never believed that she is of worth. It might be the gift of honesty in a man who has always felt compelled to practice deceptiveness. It might be deep compassion in one who tends to be self-centered.

The shadow can also be negative characteristics that we refuse to believe are a part of us, such as stubbornness, greed, jealousy, lust, hatred, or self-pity.

The negative characteristics of our shadow are not sinful any more than our flaws are sinful in themselves. These things only become sinful if we deliberately make them a source of harm for ourselves or others. Our flaws may simply be that part of us that consistently rises up unexpectedly in our lives and seems uncontrollable. It gets in our way, causes discomfort, and reminds us that we are not perfect. If we are to grow in wholeness, we need to know and claim our Shadow as much as we can.

In *Make Friends with Your Shadow*, William Miller reminds us that Jesus was one of the greatest supporters of getting to know the shadow side of our personality. He points out that Jesus' wise and insightful teachings are "an understanding of wholeness" that includes both the known and unknown, or unwanted, parts of our personality. Jesus was a promoter of truth. He often pressed others to look deeply and to discover their true identity.

What wants to come out of your shadow to help you become more whole? Are there any parts of your personality that you do not accept? How can you befriend them in order to learn more about your life?

THE DAILY PRACTICE

Breathprayer

> Breathing in: Loving Presence . . .
> Breathing out: . . . I want to grow

Reflection

Set your cup in a place where it casts a shadow, either by your candle or under a lamp.
Gaze upon the cup and its shadow.
Let what you see speak to you about your life.
Place your hand in the shadow of the cup.
Ask God to help you befriend your unknown realm and to learn from this part of yourself.

Scripture: Matthew 7:1-5

How can you say to your neighbor: "Let me take the speck out of your eye" while the log is in your own eye? (Mt 7:4).

Journaling

Write a letter, or carry on a conversation with some quality of yourself that you would rather not have.
As you reflect on the concept of "shadow," what are some of your key thoughts and emotions?
God of unconditional love . . .

Prayer

Guide and Companion of my life,
take me to the hidden places of my shadow
where both wanted and unwanted qualities dwell.
Grant me courage to face my inner enemies.
Help me to learn from them.
Fill me with light to see the undeveloped
aspects within me that long to be lived.
May I accept any goodness that I have heretofore
refused to believe is a part of myself.
Fill me with love for who I am.

Today

When I see the shadows of physical things, I will ask God to help me know and accept my inner shadow.

Day 3

The Cleansed Cup

You have many different natures. Light and dark. Kind and mean.
Inconsistent and predictable. You'll never be perfect. But you can
be better than you are now. For your own sake, try.

—Nancy Wood

One day a colleague stopped by my office to visit. As he walked in, he passed by my desk and glanced into my empty coffee cup. He looked into it, laughed, and said, "Wow, that cup is really dirty." I was startled by his comment. Later, I looked inside of it and, sure enough, it was very discolored and stained. I couldn't remember when I'd last given it a good scrubbing. That evening I took some cleansing powder and was astonished at how clean it became with a bit of attention.

Like my coffee cup, I know that I need to be regularly cleansed from inner stains that keep me from living as a loving person. My life can easily get drab, discolored, and stained with the day-to-day grime that collects when I do not pay attention on a deeper level. These stains might be old patterns of thinking or unbridled emotions that hurt myself or others, unhealthy attitudes that lash out at life instead of nurturing it, or any other dimension that brings harm to myself or to my world. A "stain" of mine that consistently collects is self-absorption. I constantly need to clean self-centeredness out of my heart so it can be filled with awareness of others.

One of the paradoxes about inner stains is that while the stains must be recognized and attended, love for one's self must continue fully. It is not the nagging, coercing, and denigrating of my spirit that will bring change. It is the knowledge that I am capable of much greater goodness that creates a desire in me to change. It has been my experience that the more I have believed in my inner storehouse of goodness, the more I have wanted to become truly loving and whole.

Another paradox is that there are some stains that can be removed and others that will remain my whole life long. I continually pray for guidance so that I will know what stains need some spiritual elbow grease and which ones are part of the "character" of my being.

I invite you to pray for an awareness of what needs cleansing within you. Ask for guidance about how to have the stains removed. Wait patiently and then accept the ways in which the scrubbing happens in such things as interruptions, challenges, feelings of love, new ideas, or unforeseen glitches in an otherwise neatly planned life.

THE DAILY PRACTICE

Breathprayer

> Breathing in: Create in me . . .
> Breathing out: . . . a clean heart, O God

Reflection

> Sit with your cup in your hands.
> Notice if your cup is stained or not.
> Ask God to help you see one inner stain of yours.
> Be still and wait for this awareness to arise.
> Whether it is stained or not, take your cup to a sink.
> Prayerfully wash it with soap and water.
> As you do so, pray to be cleansed of what sullies your spirit.

Scripture: Psalm 51

> Create in me a clean heart, O God,
> and put a new and steadfast spirit within me (Ps 51:10).
> First clean the inside of the cup,
> so that the outside also may become clean (Mt 23:26).

Journaling

> As I reflect upon my life, I see that I regularly need cleansing of
> . . . because. . .
> When I think of my stains that are irremovable, I . . .
> Thank you, God, for . . .

Prayer

Create a clean heart in me, O God. Help me to be attentive to my inner world. May I see the beauty and wonder of who I am. May I also see whatever needs to be cleansed and purified. Wash away my unloving aspects and draw me ever more closely to your love.

Today

I will be aware of my need for spiritual cleansing when I shower, wash my hands, wash dishes, etc.

Day 4

The Cup of Mercy

> The dialogue with God which begins with the confession of one's own failures is not depressing; it is liberating. At last, perhaps even for the first time, we have been honest with ourselves about what we are; and we have been honest with the one Person before whom there is no deception.
>
> —Emilie Griffin

Part of our flawed human condition is that we do sometimes fail. Beatrice Bruteau writes: "Falling is part of the journey" (*The Easter Mysteries*). *Webster's Dictionary* lists many definitions of failure: deficiency in a duty, obligation, or expectation; lack of success toward a desired end; insufficiency; falling short; not passing; entirely wanting; omitting or neglecting.

I have discovered that no matter how hard I try, I continue to fail every now and then. I still make mistakes, poor decisions, hasty judgments, and badly chosen comments. Sometimes these are intentional behaviors and sometimes I "mess up" without ever intending to do so. The blessing of failure is that it leads me to greater truth if I do not let myself drown in discouragement, regrets, or self-disparagement.

Did you ever notice the people whom Jesus called and drew to himself? They were people who failed, people who were flawed. These very ordinary people were the ones Jesus yearned to teach and to guide toward wholeness. We don't find Jesus lingering very long with people who thought they were living life perfectly. In fact, it is the ones who thought they were living perfectly (the scribes and Pharisees) whom Jesus severely reprimanded.

It is out of our human lives that God reaches us. We expect that these lives would be less wounded, less bumbling, less muddled. We hope that our lives would have a quality of "pureness" to them, but God reaches us in the way that God has always reached human beings—through our ordinary, flawed lives.

No matter what the reason for our failures, we need to eventually move to the place where we forgive ourselves for how we have failed. We also need to ask forgiveness of God and of others if we have harmed them. And then we turn with trust to the One who readily and endlessly extends the cup of mercy to us. The scriptures are very clear about God's welcome of us, even when we feel like the greatest failure in the world.

Look at your flawed life today and let God come into it.

THE DAILY PRACTICE

Breathprayer

> Breathing in: Held in your mercy . . .
> Breathing out: . . . held in your love

Reflection

> Remember one of the failures of your life.
> Write a word for this failure on a small piece of paper.
> Place this paper in your cup, symbolic of your self.
> Hold the cup in your hands.
> Notice any emotions you have as you hold the failure.
> Speak to God about your thoughts and emotions.
> Ask to receive God's understanding and mercy.
> Listen quietly to God's response.
>
> Then take out the piece of paper and tear it to shreds as a sign of your letting go of this failure.

Scripture: Psalm 25

> Be mindful of your mercy . . .
> and of your steadfast love,
> for they have been from of old (Ps 25:6).

Journaling

> One failure I still need to forgive myself for is . . .
> What do you think and feel about your failures? Have you changed because of them? If so, how?
> God of mercy . . .

Wellspring of Mercy, you welcome me home.
You understand my human failings.
You embrace me in my incompleteness.
You help me move on from failures and defeat.
How good and gracious is your kindness to me.

Today

___

I will greet myself mercifully at least once today.

___

Day 5

Which Cup Is Best?

Inside the Great Mystery that is,
we don't really own anything.
What is this competition we feel then,
before we go, one at a time, through the same gate?

—Rumi

I can see her clearly. Her name was Shirley Kolmer, an American member of the Precious Blood religious community. I met her in Liberia where she was working at a local high school. Shirley was a vibrant woman with lovely white hair. When she smiled one could easily see the gap between her upper front teeth. In the United States most people would have rushed her to the orthodontist for braces to correct the situation. Not in Liberia. In that culture, a gap in one's front teeth is a sign of great beauty. When I discovered that, I thought of how easily we are seduced by our cultural expectations into what is or is not acceptable.

Yet, I see and hear this all the time—constant comparisons and competitions based on what our culture tells us is good looking, attractive, desirous, etc. People end up rejecting themselves or others because they might not have all the "correct" standards and qualifications. It is not just external looks that are part of the competition; there is also competition for who is the best in spiritual growth. People envy others for their "holiness" or their ability to pray instead of valuing the way that God is moving uniquely in their own lives. It is very difficult to be ourselves and not be shaped by the expectations of others.

We aren't meant to be like everyone else, although we constantly hear this expectation. This same culture instills in us the idea that there's something wrong with us—we are flawed—if we don't measure up to certain qualifications. Maybe that's why so many people envy others' bodies, intelligence, personality traits, or talents. We tend to consistently sit in judgment upon ourselves and upon others. This is dangerous for the spiritual life. In her book, *On the Wings of Self Esteem*, Louise Hart warns: "Comparison sets us up for unhealthy competition. It drives wedges between people, creates separation, and enforces conformity." When we consistently compare ourselves with others, we can end up rejecting our selves—God's beloved creatures—and we follow someone else's dream instead of our own.

Today give thanks to God for all you are and have. Do not heed the false voices of your culture.

THE DAILY PRACTICE

Breathprayer

> Breathing in: I am (your name) . . .
> Breathing out: . . . thank you, God

Reflection

> Find another cup and set it beside yours.
> Sit quietly, looking at the two cups.
> Enjoy the uniqueness of each cup.
> Reflect on your own originality.
> Think of yourself with others.

Bring any comparison and competition to God.
Listen to God's message to you.
Offer gratitude to God for who you are.

Scripture: Romans 9:19-26

But who indeed are you, a human being, to argue with God? Will what is molded say to the one who molds it, "Why have you made me like this?" Has the potter no right over the clay, to make out of the same lump one object for special use and another for ordinary use? (Rom 9:20-21).

Journaling

I fall into the trap of competition and comparison when . . .
When I reflect on my own uniqueness, I . . .
Dear Creator . . .

Prayer

When I look longingly at the gifts of others and forget or deny my own gifts from you, God, lead me to accept myself as I am. When I constantly compare myself to another, grant me an appreciation for my own distinct personhood. When I get caught in envy, jealousy, gossip, or rejection of myself or others, draw me back to you and teach me more about the love you have for each of us.

Today

I will not envy others or compete with them.

Day 6

The Cup of Wisdom

To the holy people she [Holy Wisdom] gave the wages of their labors; she guided them by a marvelous road, herself their shelter by day—and their starlight through the night.

—Wisdom 10:17

During the past five days, I have often mentioned the need for guidance as we look at our less-than-perfect lives. It is easy to deceive ourselves as we walk on our spiritual path. Because we are flawed human creatures, we can get side-tracked. We can lose our focus and get caught in huge self-improvement programs of our own making that have little to do with God's desires for us. We can become absorbed in trying to be someone other than our own true selves. We can forget that we are never without access to a Loving Being who regards us with great tenderness and is always walking with us.

We need wisdom so that we will know when to embrace our imperfect selves with compassion and when to give our imperfect selves a swift kick in the right direction. Divine guidance is a source of wisdom for us that helps us to know when to embrace ourselves and when to not give in to ourselves. Guidance implies that someone knows the way, a Wise One who is willing to walk with us. Guidance gives us the opportunity to listen to someone who has much more wisdom than we do.

Guidance is about hearing the inner voice in us that keeps us closely connected with God's ways, giving us direction for our lives. It's not that our lives are all mapped out for us by God. The path is rarely a clear, visible, neatly defined one. No, rather, Divine Wisdom helps us to discover, each step of the way, how we are to be a loving person in our world with our chipped, flawed condition.

Direction for one's spiritual path has always been a need of people who are intent on following God's ways. Many of the psalms ask God to show the way. One of the biblical names for our guiding God is Holy Wisdom. It is this Wisdom who led the Hebrew people through the wilderness of their lives when they were wandering and wondering in what direction to turn. It is this Wisdom who gave them shelter by day and starlight by night so that they could find their way.

Let us trust in this wonderful guide who has also been given to us. Let us turn often to ask for guidance and direction for our spiritual path for we, too, need this Wise One to teach us how to be and where to go.

THE DAILY PRACTICE

Breathprayer

> Breathing in: Send your light . . .
> Breathing out: . . . send your truth

Reflection

> Hold your cup in your hands.
> Recall that you are held in the Wise Hands of God.
> As a sign of the all-encompassing guidance and wisdom of God in your life, very slowly and reflectively turn your cup to each of the four directions of the room.
> After each turn of the cup, pray Psalm 43:3:
> "O send out your light and your truth, let them lead me."

Scripture: Psalm 16

> I bless God who gives me counsel,
> in the night, also, my heart instructs me.
> I keep God always before me (Ps 16:7-8).

Journaling

> The area in which I most sense that I need God's guidance is . . .
> I have known the presence of Holy Wisdom when . . .
> Dear Wise One . . .

O Holy Wisdom,
as I walk the spiritual path
with my chipped and flawed condition,
guide and direct my life.
May I make good choices that are
reflective of the loving goodness
of you, my God.

Today

———

I will call on Holy Wisdom at least twice during the day and ask
for guidance.

———

Day 7

Integration/Review

1. Visit and review your past six days.

2. Highlight anything in your journal that particularly touches you
   with its truth.

3. Write a brief summary of this week. (Alternatives for this summary
   would be to use paints, clay, dance, or you could draw a cup and let
   the size, shape, form, contents, and message on it symbolize what
   you experienced this week.)

Memo

How is your experience of journaling? Remember that you do not need
to respond to all three of the suggestions for journaling. Choose one that
best fits your current situation.

Also, be kind to yourself and do not judge the quality of what you have written by whether it sounds inspirational or poetic. Journaling is not about writing well—it is about connecting and integrating what we have prayed and recording it for memory's sake as well as for greater clarification. Do not let yourself be fooled into thinking your journaling is worthless or inadequate because it does not meet your criteria for great writing!

THE BROKEN CUP

A View of the Week

I have become like a broken vessel.

—Psalm 31:12

I was offering a Lenten retreat day based on the image of the cup and had just stopped speaking in order to take a morning coffee break with the group. I looked up and there, coming toward the podium, was a woman in her early fifties. She was wobbling, leaning heavily on a five-pronged cane, her head shaking from side to side. When she came up to me I could barely understand her speech. She tried to tell me how a severe asthma attack caused a coma that left her with brain damage. This brave, wounded woman had begun learning to talk and walk all over again.

She had struggled to walk to the front of the room to tell me about the cup she had brought with her. She said she had no idea what the day was about other than that she was to bring a cup with her. Then she showed me her cup. The handle had been broken off leaving two sharp poking edges in its place. I gasped. It couldn't have been a better symbol for what had recently happened to her.

The broken cup reminds me of those times when hurts, wounds, pains, and adversities of all sorts invade our lives and change us forever. During these times, all we can do is try to survive, slowly recover, and start anew. It is often difficult for us to give or to receive during this brokenness. The pain knocks us over, like a cup on its side. We may feel like all our hope has been drained out of our lives. When the cup of our lives is broken apart, it has to have the pieces put back together again.

Sometimes the brokenness is not so severe. It may consist of smaller, daily obstacles and irritations. The pieces of our lives may be troubles that go on and on with no end in sight, constant physical pain, negative moods, or unhealthy habits. Whatever the difficulty that we experience, it can be a source of our spiritual growth. So much depends on how we view these pieces of brokenness and what we do or do not do with them.

Our brokenness can be an instrument for change. Pain received rightly has the power to transform our lives. Madeleine L'Engle writes: "I look back at my mother's life and I see suffering deepening and strengthening it. In some people I have also seen it destroy. Pain is not always creative; received wrongly, it can lead to alcoholism and madness and suicide. Nevertheless, without it we do not grow" (*Walking On Water*).

What would happen if we met our frustrations, pains, and heartaches as we would meet a visitor having something to teach us? What if we lingered a bit with our brokenness and asked it to help us to grow? What might we learn from those pieces of our lives that are still wanting and incomplete?

Each day of this week you are invited to ponder some aspect of your brokenness—that part of your life that empties you or fragments you—to discover how it has been, or can be, a teacher for your growth. It is also a week to find comfort as you pray about the strength and shelter of God and to deepen your hope as you reflect on aspects of healing.

As you begin your prayer each day, *turn the cup on its side to remind you of the pain and powerlessness of being broken.* Let the cup stay that way unless the day's prayer indicates otherwise. Also, *put a seed or a packet of seeds by your cup for this week.* Let it remind you of how the seed's husk must be broken open before the green shoot comes forth. May it also remind you of the power for personal growth that is within your difficult times.

As you ponder your life experiences of brokenness this week, I encourage you to carry this message of Anne Lamott in your heart: "Hope begins in the dark, the stubborn hope that if you just show up and try to do the right thing, the dawn will come. You wait and watch and work, and you don't give up."

Love pours out
but the broken cup
cannot receive

too pained
too discouraged
too shamed
too brokenhearted
too burned out
too lonely
too disenchanted

Love waits to strengthen
Love waits to nourish
Love waits to be received
Love waits to heal

in time
the cup will be mended
in time
the cup will be raised
in time
the cup will receive again

in time
in time

—Joyce Rupp

Day 1

Joy and Sorrow

The most helpful discovery of today has been that right in the midst of my sorrows there is always room for joy. Joy and sorrow are sisters; they live in the same house.

—Macrina Wiederkehr

I recently walked the spiritual journey with a woman who was in deep depression for many months. She couldn't think straight, had no energy and was assaulted constantly with negative thoughts about herself. One day she found enough strength to listen to her suffering. When she did so, she heard within it the call to be less controlling about her life. Being in control and always showing strength was an old message from her family that she had tried to live for many years. The day she really listened to her pain, the pieces of her cup of life began to teach her, and she started to mend.

She learned that life will not always be to her liking, that there is a natural cycle of the spirit similar to the earth's cycle of seasons. Just as the trees have their seasons of blooming and barrenness, just as the land has its fruitful time and its fallow time, so does the human spirit. There will be winter times when her spirit feels empty and her life seems fruitless. There will also be the summer times when a sense of satisfaction and joy will prevail in her spirit. She learned that these seasons will come and go in spite of how much effort she might give to having only joy in her life.

Feeling powerless and vulnerable taught her that she could not always control every aspect of her life no matter how hard she tried. She learned that it took more effort to fight against the unwanted inner visitors than it did to listen to them. The memory of her brokenness helped her to accept the balance of life with its joy and its sorrow. She's freer now and much more at peace. Difficult things still happen, but now she knows that these things are a part of the life cycle, and that they will eventually pass. She knows that joy and sorrow are both a part of the process of growth. She understands that each has something significant to bring into her life.

Pause today to look at your history of inner seasons. Is it possible for you to accept the difficult seasons along with the joyful ones, to see each as an essential part of your spiritual growth?

THE DAILY PRACTICE

Breathprayer

> Breathing in: Joy and sorrow . . .
> Breathing out: . . . live together

Reflection

> Pick up your cup and look inside.
> Visualize a deep joy of yours in the cup.
> Now, visualize a deep pain of yours also in the cup.
> Let these two be there, intermingled into oneness.
> Hold the cup to your heart.
> Let this gesture be a willingness of yours to accept and to learn from both joy and sorrow.

Scripture: John 12:20-26; John 16:25-33

> Very truly, I tell you, unless a grain of wheat falls into the earth and dies, it remains just a single grain; but if it dies, it bears much fruit (Jn 12:24).

> You will have pain, but your pain will turn into joy (Jn 16:20).

Journaling

> Ask Jesus: "What helped you in your difficult times?"
> Listen. Write what he responds to this question.
> Joy and sorrow have taught me . . .
> When I consider "listening to my pain," I . . .

_____

God of joy and sorrow, help me to do less judging of my life experiences as "good" or "bad" and to do more receiving of them as a part of the process of spiritual growth. I trust that you will be my faithful companion and that you will strengthen me during my difficult times. Help me to grow through all of the seasons of my life.

Today

_____

I will look for and listen to what joy and sorrow are teaching me.

_____

Day 2

The Cup of Suffering

Are you able to drink the cup that I am about to drink?

—Matthew 20:22

When the mother of the sons of Zebedee came to Jesus and asked that they be given special places in his kingdom, Jesus responded by using the symbol of the cup, referring to the suffering of his passion and death. Jesus was saying with the cup, "There is a consequence if you make a choice to be with me. If you want the glory of being with me, you'll have to take the suffering, too." Jesus was speaking of the challenge and the struggle to live a life of love as he had lived it. He was reminding them that discipleship is no easy thing.

Each of our life choices, decisions, and actions involves some consequences. Something will happen because of what we think, say, and do. These consequences may bring gladness, but they may also bring sadness.

For example, if we choose to love someone deeply, we must be willing to accept that our heart's investment may cost us loneliness and heartache. We will be challenged to accept that person's weaknesses as well as that person's strengths. We may bear deep sorrow if he or she dies or chooses to leave us without our consent.

Every investment has a consequence. Those who have children know the gift of these wonderful beings, but they also know the tremendous sacrifices involved. Physicians know the satisfaction of helping a patient to heal, but they also pay the price of long, intense hours of work that often infringe on their family life. For myself, as a writer, I love the "glory" of seeing words come together, but I must also accept the pain of the writing process—loneliness, editing, deadlines, and vulnerability. At some time or other, we all have to face the question that Jesus asked his disciples. We ought not to run from the question because it contains within it the seed of spiritual growth.

Even Jesus found the consequences of his commitment difficult. In the Garden of Gethsemane, he begged to have the cup of suffering pass from him. Still, he found the inner strength to say yes to what was asked of him. With each part of our life we can ask ourselves: Am I willing to accept the pain that my investment may cost me? Am I ready to be generous with my commitment even if it brings suffering my way? In other words, am I willing to walk in the footsteps of Jesus?

THE DAILY PRACTICE

Breathprayer

> Breathing in: Strengthen me . . .
> Breathing out: . . . encourage me

Reflection

> Lift the cup turned sideways from the table.
> Hold it in your hands, still turned on its side.
> Think about your life choices and commitments.
> Which ones have brought, or are bringing, pain to you?

As you hold the cup, hold the pain which comes as a consequence of your choices and decisions.
Open your inner being to the Beloved.
Receive the power you need to accept the consequences of your choices.

Scripture: Mark 8:34-38

If any want to become my followers, let them deny themselves, take up their cross and follow me (Mk 8:34).

Journaling

One of the joys about my life-choice is . . .
One of the sorrows about my life-choice is . . .
When I read the scripture verse about taking up my cross, I . . .

Prayer

Jesus, happiness and struggle were constantly woven through your life. Why is it that I want the joy, the glory, the good stuff, but I don't want the sorrow, the pain, the struggle? Strengthen me and guide me when crosses such as anxiety, struggle, heartache, loneliness, sadness, time-crunches, and frustrations pervade my days. Deepen my desire to be your disciple.

Today

Each time I take a drink of any liquid, I will say yes to the consequences of my life-choice and decisions.

Day 3

My Cup of Tears

How large a cup of tears must I drink, O God?
How much is enough?

—Ann Weems

A nn Weems' *Psalms of Lament* come straight from the deep heartache of her son's death. Her psalms, based on the psalms of the Hebrew scriptures, are honest, gutsy, keening cries of distress. These prayers remind me that through the ages, hurting people have raised their anguished voices to God. These voices have been filled with questions, demands, accusations, and beseechments. They have implored, begged, and pleaded with God.

I used to be too nice with God when I was feeling like a broken cup. I realize now that not being honest with God about my situation only added to my anger and hostility. Keeping it all inside, trying to hide it, benefited no one and only generated more self-pity and resentment. I do not believe that God sends suffering. Suffering happens because of our human condition and because of the way that transformation occurs with its natural cycle of life-death-life. Still, this reality does not take away my human emotional response when pain is intensely penetrating nor does it eliminate my hope that God will somehow choose a miracle on my behalf.

The Jewish psalms have taught me a lot about how to pray when life is tough. The psalmist yells, screams, and pokes a finger at God now and then in accusatory blame. The psalmist wonders why God isn't making some changes. Once the emotional tirade of woes is over, another equally valuable part of the prayer comes. The psalmist closes by expressing confidence and hope in God, trusting that all shall eventually be well. The prayer style of the psalms assures me of how good it is to be honest with myself, as well as with God, and to count on God's healing presence to eventually bring me peace of mind and heart.

Every nook and cranny of our lives, no matter how painful, deserves God's attention. Psalm 56 addresses God with this reassurance: "You have . . . put my tears in your bottle" (Ps 56:8). In other words, God gathers our pain and struggle and holds them compassionately. It is good to bring God our tears. God can catch them and hold them with care until we find our inner peace again.

THE DAILY PRACTICE

Breathprayer

> Breathing in: Hold me . . .
> Breathing out: . . . in your love

Reflection

> Hold the cup upright in your hands.
> Look upon it as a cup that holds tears.
> Let the cup represent your own pain and tears or the pain and tears of someone you know.
> Envision God's hands around your hands as you hold the cup of tears.
> Allow this Compassionate Presence to give comfort to you or to another who is in pain.

Scripture: Revelation 7:13-17; Jeremiah 31:1-14

> And God will wipe away every tear from their eyes (Rev 7:17).
>
> I will turn their mourning into joy, I will comfort them (Jer 31:13).

Journaling

> Draw the cup of your tears, with teardrops falling into the cup. On the teardrops, write words that tell of your pain.
> How have you experienced God when you have been deep into the tough things of life?
> Comforting One . . .

Prayer (to be prayed for yourself or for another in pain)

> Sheltering Presence, come with your comforting embrace and catch my tears with your compassionate love. Be near with your

protecting refuge. Heal the place within me that cries out to be freed from pain. Hold me close to you and hear my yearning for peace.

When I use a cup or a glass, I will be aware of how God catches the tears of those who hurt and holds them with care.

Day 4

The Unmendable Cup

Both my parents died without any reconciliation between us. I, their only child, did not live up to their expectations. Nor did they to mine. I wish it had not been so, and they must have felt the same way. The ritual of reunion never happened. The distance between us was so great that I didn't even attend their funerals.

—Robert Fulghum

Sometimes there are parts of our lives that are unmendable. Like the old Humpty Dumpty rhyme, we cannot always put the pieces of our life back together again, at least not in the same way that they were before. Some pieces are irreplaceable or unable to be "fixed." Closed institutions, lost jobs, shattered relationships, loved ones who have died, dreams never brought to birth, and permanent bodily changes from disease, aging, or accidents are all situations that cannot be restored.

It was too late for Robert Fulghum to mend the relationship with his parents because they had died, but not too late for him to mend his own heart and to come to some inner reconciliation. So too for us. Although we may not be able to put the old pieces of a situation, event, or experience back together again, we can still mend our spirits.

Old hurts, heartaches, memories, destructive behaviors, and other wounds do not have to break us apart forever. The Serenity Prayer expresses this vital truth—we need wisdom to know when something is mendable and when it is irreparable. We need courage to take the necessary steps to move on with our lives, whether those steps are leaving someone or something behind, or returning to the brokenness and taking action to put the pieces back together again.

When our woundedness involves a situation that cannot be mended, then there comes a time when we have to cease our attempts to put those pieces of our life together. The healing of our spirit will come when we let go of the past, stop trying to have things be as they used to be, get on with our lives, and tend to what is before us.

Today can be a day to take inventory of your life to see if there are any fragments that cannot be mended and, if so, to give them your goodbye.

THE DAILY PRACTICE

Breathprayer

> Breathing in: Let the past be . . .
> Breathing out: . . . let the past be

Reflection

> Ponder the cup as it lays on its side before you.
> Is there anything in your life that seems unable to "rise up"?
> Think about the possibility of it not being mendable.
> Are you at peace with letting go of it?
> Ask God for what you need in order to be healed.
> Pick up the cup and hold it, upright, in your hands.
>
> Ask God to give you wisdom and courage to let go of any old pain and difficulties that keep you in bondage.

> Do not remember the former things,
> or consider the things of old.
> I am about to do a new thing;
> now it springs forth,
> do you not perceive it? (Is 43:18-19).

Journaling

Pieces of my life that I cannot "fix" and need to leave behind
are . . .
Write a dialogue with a part of your "broken" past.
Dear God, please grant me wisdom to know . . .

Prayer

God, grant me the serenity
to accept the things I cannot change,
the courage to change the things I can,
and the wisdom to know the difference.

—The Serenity Prayer

Today

I will let go of one of the pieces of my past that cannot be mended.

Day 5

Recognizing Resistances

I am entirely ready to have the chains that keep me bound be broken. I am entirely ready for the walls I've built around myself to be torn down. I am entirely ready to give up my need to control every situation. I am entirely ready to let go of my resentments. I am entirely ready to grow up.

—Macrina Wiederkehr

One of the most powerful teaching stories I have ever read is told in Jack Kornfield's book *A Path With Heart*. A father is away from home when robbers come, set fire to the house, and take his young son away with them. The father returns to the ashes of his house and believes his son has died there. He grieves uncontrollably for many months. The son manages to get free from his abductors and find his way home. He knocks on the door and cries "Papa, Papa," but the father refuses to open the door, thinking it is one of the neighborhood children taunting him. Eventually the son goes away, never to return.

In this story, the father resists the truth that can bring him joy and freedom from his loss because he clings so much to what he thinks is the truth. When we are in pain, we can easily live with illusions. We may think such things as "No one loves me. No one cares. I will never feel happy again. It was all my fault. I can't do that. I don't know enough yet," etc. The beginning of healing may be there, but we refuse to let it in because of our resistance.

Our resistance can take many other forms as well. They might be a silent withdrawal, apathy, running away, talking incessantly, defending and challenging, constantly being busy, ignoring or pretending not to understand, being critical, or making excuses. Resistance is like placing a hand over the opening to a cup. Nothing can come into or be poured out of the cup. So, too, with our spiritual life.

Martha, the sister of Lazarus, did not believe her brother Lazarus could be restored to life. She insisted that he had been dead too long. Martha resisted the possibility that Jesus could call him out of his tomb of deadness. Is there anything in your life that you think cannot be restored to life? Are there any blocks to your spiritual growth?

THE DAILY PRACTICE

Breathprayer

> Breathing in: Let go . . .
> Breathing out: . . . let go

Reflection

> Hold your cup in your hands.
> Place one hand over the open space of the cup.
> Reflect on your resistances and refusals.
> How do these block your openness to growth?
> Picture yourself held in God's hands.
> Loosen your grip on your worries and insecurities.
> Listen to God speak to you about trust.
> Take your hand off your cup.
> Notice how ready it is now to receive.
> Hold the cup to your heart.
> Stand and make a deep bow as a sign of your surrender to God.

Scripture: John 11:1-44

> Jesus said, "Take away the stone." Martha, the sister of the dead man, said to him, "Lord, already there is a stench because he has been dead four days" (Jn 11:39).

Journaling

> One excuse I often give for not growing spiritually is . . .
> I cling to and clutch onto . . . I push away . . .
> Dear Life-Giver . . .

___

God of truth, help me to discover my resistances to my growth. Shine your light on my illusions. Uncover my fears. Reveal my strongholds. Soften my grip on my security. Open my closedness. Lead me to greater freedom and inner healing.

Today
___

I will notice the excuses I make for avoiding things that I dislike doing, and then I will do one of these things that I dislike.

Day 6

The Mended Cup

Waiting is endless. . . . I wait because I am powerless to do anything else. I wait because what I most treasure is what is deepest within and protected by silence. Out of waiting comes patience. Out of accepting my powerlessness comes strength and love and the courage to dare.

—**Christin Lore Weber**

During one of the years that I lived at a Benedictine monastery, I saw my first pregnant llama on the monastery farm. I was so excited. Every day I looked at Mama Llama to see if the baby had come. One day I was walking over to the monastery and I saw that Mama Llama was tied to a tree on the lawn where she often grazed. Then I saw the new one. She was clean, snow-white, with dry, fluffy wool. I felt disappointed that I had missed the birthing. I wondered when she had been born, and I asked the sisters at the monastery about the birth. "What baby llama?!" they exclaimed, and all went running out to see. Lo and behold, the baby had just been born there on the lawn and I didn't even know it! I had assumed that the baby was at least a day old because I didn't know how quickly newborn llamas are ready to run with the herd.

Later that day I thought, "That's like healing. I wait and wait for something to happen and then I don't even recognize it when it does happen." Healing takes a lot of patience and much time. Like a deep wound in the body that heals from the inside out, so with our spiritual healing. We may not always readily see the steady healing occurring, but we need to believe that the mending is taking place.

Besides believing that we can be healed, our mending also requires:

- naming and working with our unwanted emotions
- extending compassion toward ourselves and others
- letting go of resistances
- trusting and yielding to God
- receiving support from others
- extending and receiving forgiveness
- taking good care of our body and our spirit

We may not be able to undo or fix the past, but we can be healed from what has wounded us. Today is a good day to remember that healing is a process, not a one-time event. Let us patiently approach the process of our inner healing with trust and with confidence.

THE DAILY PRACTICE

Breathprayer

> Breathing in: Healing God . . .
> Breathing out: . . . I hope in you

Reflection

> Turn the cup sideways in your hands.
> Picture your old wounds and hurts in it.
> Mentally take them out, one by one.

Put them into the Divine Healer's hands.
Now hold the cup upright in your hands.
Think about the broken pieces that have been mended.
Thank God for these mending times.
Ask for patience and hope.

Scripture: Ezekiel 34:11-16

> I will seek the lost,
> and I will bring back the strayed,
> and I will bind up the injured,
> and I will strengthen the weak (Ez 34:16).

Journaling

What aspect of healing is easiest for me? What aspect of healing is most difficult or challenging?
Write your own life version of "Amazing Grace."
Dialogue with one of the mended parts of your life (or with one of the wounded parts that is still in the process of being healed).

Prayer

God of healing, help me to mend the broken places of my life. Direct my mind and heart to sources of hope and healing. Let me not forget all that remains for me as I ponder what has gone from my life. Be my vision and my strength. Anoint me with the oil of your love and take my hand as I move forward into ever greater healing.

Today

I will wear a Band-Aid as a sign of my trust in God to heal whatever is broken in my life and as a thank you for what has already been healed.

Day 7

Integration/Review

1. Visit and review your past six days.

2. Highlight anything in your journal that particularly touches you with its truth.

3. Write a brief summary of this week. (Alternatives to writing would be to use paints, clay, dance, or you could draw a cup and let the size, shape, form, contents, and message on it symbolize what you experienced this week.)

Memo

How is your time of "Reflection" with the cup? You might be finding this to be an easy and enjoyable part of the daily practice, or you might be having a difficult time with it. For some, using images and visualization is a painful process. If this is true for you, do not be concerned about "seeing" something. Just get a sense of what is being envisioned. Don't try too hard; let the thoughts and feelings unfold in your own way. Let God lead you.

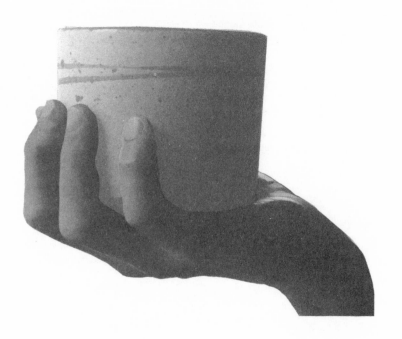

Week V

THE CUP OF COMPASSION

Day 1: Learning Compassion
Day 2: Offering the Cup
Day 3: Giving the Cup Freely
Day 4: The Cup of Sacrifice
Day 5: Pouring from the Cup
Day 6: The Gift of Be-ing
Day 7: Integration/Review

A View of the Week

I hold my heart as a gourd filled with love, ready to pour upon humanity.

—Jessica Powers

One Thursday when I was visiting at Kavanaugh House, a residence for terminally ill persons, I met a woman named Agnes. She was sitting by the bedside of her husband, Al, who had a brain tumor. The next Thursday I again found Agnes faithfully sitting there by Al. This time she told me about Marian, a woman whose husband had died at Kavanaugh House the week before. Agnes knew Marian only from a few conversations they had before Marian's husband died. This new widow understood what Agnes was going through and wanted to support her. She began calling Agnes each evening to see how she was coping. Agnes told me how much the phone calls helped her to get through each day. As the weeks unfolded, I saw how one woman, in the midst of her own loss, reached out in compassion to another who was in pain. Marian couldn't "do" much for Agnes by changing her situation, but she helped greatly with her caring presence.

Mary Jo Meadows defines compassion as "the quivering of the heart in response to another's suffering" and notes that "compassionate beings . . . cannot bear to see suffering and remain unengaged." Compassion is the quality of being able to "get inside the skin of another" in order to respond with loving concern and care. Jack Kornfield writes about the truly loving person breathing in the pain of the world and breathing out compassion. That is how deep compassion is, and how closely connected it is to others.

Each life influences and affects others in some way. The more we see our world as a vast interconnectedness of all beings, the more drawn we will be to compassion because we will see how much one life is related to and affected by another. This spiritual oneness is at the heart of Christianity. Christ is the vine, and we are the branches. We are the body of Christ (Jn 15; 1 Cor 12). The life pulsing through us is the life of God giving us spiritual vitality.

Probably no quality more identifies a Christian than that of compassion. Read through a gospel and you will find that Jesus consistently lived this quality and encouraged it in his disciples. He repeatedly insisted that offering compassion to another was the same as extending it to himself.

Compassion can be very demanding. It is not easy to know the pain and to feel the hurt of another. Sometimes compassion asks us to simply "be" with someone, to wait patiently, to experience their powerlessness with them. At other times, compassion asks us to "do" something, to give of our time and resources, to speak out for justice, to "go the extra mile" for and with them as did the Samaritan in the gospel parable. And sometimes, compassion asks us to receive graciously from another who has need of our receptivity and our vulnerability.

Caring persons need to constantly check their motivation for offering compassion to be sure they are not doing it out of their own egocentric needs. They must also be sure to take good care of themselves. As Mary Jo Meadows points out, "You must get near enough to suffering to feel it, but not so close as to get lost in it or overwhelmed by it." This can be a very delicate balance.

Scripture scholar Marcus Borg notes that compassion is the central quality of God in both the Hebrew and the Christian scriptures. Borg emphasizes that God is compassionate—God feels our pain, our loss, and our suffering. As we pray with our cups this week, we can draw both inspiration and comfort from God who is our example, *par excellence*, of how to hold the hurting ones of our world in our hearts and offer them the cup of compassion.

my cup of compassion
holds tears of the world;
it overflows with sorrow,
struggles, and sadness.

my cup of compassion
holds the cries of children,
unfed, unloved, unsheltered,
uneducated, unwanted.

my cup of compassion
holds the screams of war,
the tortured, slain,
imprisoned,
the raped, the disabled.

my cup of compassion
holds the bruised and battered,
victims of incest and abuse,
gang wars, violent crimes.

my cup of compassion
holds the voice of silent ones,
the mentally ill,
illegal immigrants,
the unborn, the homeless.

my cup of compassion
holds the emptiness of the poor,
the searing pain of racism,
the impotency of injustice.

my cup of compassion
holds the heartache of loss,
the sigh of the dying,
the sting of the divorced.

my cup of compassion
holds the agony of the earth,
species terminated,
air polluted,
land destroyed,
rivers with refuse.

my cup of compassion
I hold it to my heart
where the Divine dwells,
where love is stronger
than death and disaster.

—Joyce Rupp

Day 1

Learning Compassion

What can we do? We can become a sign. Whatever happens, become a sign of joy and a fountain of divine love.

—Bede Griffiths, O.S.B.

I learned a lot about compassion from one of my college professors. I remember how surprised I was when she took a personal interest in me, a homesick freshman. I observed her care and concern for each of the students in her large classes. She would take time to stop a student in class or on campus, ask how he or she was, and then really listen to the response. I remember nothing of what she taught me in that class, but I remember everything of how she was with me and with the other students.

Compassionate people often inspire others to be compassionate. I feel this way whenever I meditate on the life of Jesus. I marvel at how Jesus was so consistently compassionate when he met the ill, the grieving, the hungry, the oppressed. He is often described as being "deeply moved in spirit" or feeling compassion for the people. Jesus touched torn and tattered people with an amazing awareness of their woundedness. The vastness of his ability to love and be loved is phenomenal.

I've also been inspired by compassionate people in history such as Dorothy Day, Mahatma Ghandi, Etty Hillisum, Tom Dooley, Mother Teresa, and Albert Schwietzer. I was in awe as I read about the English spiritual writer, Caryll Houselander. Psychologists would bring their mentally and emotionally ill patients whom they could not cure to live with Caryll because they were astounded at the effect her compassionate presence had on them. Caryll accepted and loved the patients, and this made a dramatic healing impact on their health.

When I look at the lives of compassionate people, I see some common characteristics. They often have significant suffering or painful life events of their own, a generous heart, a non-blaming and non-judging mind, a passionate spirit, a willingness to sacrifice their life, a keen empathy, and a love that embraces the oneness of all creation.

I invite you to think about your teachers of compassion today. Who has taught you how to offer the cup of compassion to others?

THE DAILY PRACTICE

Breathprayer

Breathing in: Divine Compassion . . .
Breathing out: . . . teach me

Reflection

Remember compassionate people you have known (personally or from history, scripture, literature, etc.).
Review their lives. Notice how they lived.
How did they respond compassionately?
Write down their names on a piece of paper.
Place this paper under your cup as a symbol of how their example is a base for your compassion.
Let it be a way of honoring these compassionate beings.

Scripture: Matthew 10:40-42

. . . And whoever gives even a cup of water to one of these little ones in the name of a disciple—truly I tell you, none of these will lose their reward (Mt 10:42).

Journaling

My experience of compassion . . .
The key thing that I have learned from compassionate people is . . .
God of compassion . . .

Prayer

God of hurting ones, thank you for the loving people you have brought into my life, who gave me comfort and strength in my times of pain. Thank you for my teachers of compassion and for what I have learned from them. I long to be a more compassionate person so that my life will truly reflect you. Revive and renew the gift of compassion in my life.

<u>Today</u>

I will live as a compassionate person.

Day 2

Offering the Cup

There now flows a constant stream of tenderness, a stream in which all petty desires seem to have been extinguished. All that matters now is to be kind to each other with all the goodness that is in us.

—Etty Hillisum

I don't hear much about it anymore, but I think that the image of the Body of Christ is still vital and helpful when it comes to living compassionately. This Christian spirituality envisions each of us as a part of the whole, with the Spirit of Jesus uniting us. Scripture contains images of this unity, particularly in the description of the one body that has many members: "If one member suffers, all suffer together with it; if one member is honored, all rejoice together with it" (1 Cor 12:26). Each and every part of the whole has significance and worth.

I find great strength in knowing that I am connected to everyone and everything in my world because of the vibrancy of the Divine Presence dwelling in each of us and because of the atoms that twirl and whirl in every piece of creation. All of life is a part of me, and I am a part of all of life. All people are my sisters and brothers. In each one I recognize the face of the Divine Presence looking back at me. The God of compassion has shown me a loving face; now I am to be that reflection in return. I am to be the presence of God to another. When I offer the cup of compassion to someone, it is God in me reaching to God in the other. There is a oneness of Love bonding us to all of life.

It is not only Christians who are encouraged to be a light for others and a source of love. Compassion is a core element of other religious traditions as well. In his last words to his disciples, the Buddha said, "Make of yourselves a light." How similar are the words of Jesus when he asked his followers to not hide their light under a basket but to place it where all could see. Like Jesus, the Buddha also encouraged his followers to be persons of great love.

One way of being a light or a sign of God's great compassion is by praying for and with others. Each morning I name to God the significant people of my life. I also name the groups I will be with for conferences or retreats in the coming weeks. I then pray the adapted prayer of John Cardinal Newman which I've suggested as your prayer today. In this way I am daily reminded of my oneness with others and of the call to be the messenger of God's love in all I am and all I do.

THE DAILY PRACTICE

Breathprayer

> Breathing in: We are many . . .
> Breathing out: . . . we are one

Reflection

> Hold your cup out in front of you.
> Stand and face the east.
> Unite with all beings of the east.
> Let your heart extend compassion to them.
> Turn and face the south.
> Hold your cup out to all who dwell in the south.
> Unite with these beings.
> Let your heart extend compassion to them.
> (Continue in like manner with the west and the north.)

Scripture: 1 Corinthians 12:12-31

> For just as the body is one and has many members, and all the members of the body, though many, are one body so it is with Christ. . . . Now you are the body of Christ and individually members of it (1 Cor 12:27).

Journaling

> I am a fountain of God's love when . . .
> I hesitate, or refuse, to offer the cup of compassion to . . . because . . .
> Dialogue with an individual or a group toward whom you feel biased or prejudiced.

Prayer (adapted from the prayer of John Cardinal Newman)

> Dear God, help me to spread your love everywhere I go. Penetrate and possess my whole being so fully that all my life will reflect your compassion. Shine through me and be so in me that every person I meet will feel your presence in my spirit.

Today

> I will intentionally offer compassion to someone I know who is in need of my understanding, kindness, and care.

Day 3

Giving the Cup Freely

Too many of us consent, or are forced, to spend time doing
things for which we have no heartfelt reason. If we were asked,
"Why are you doing this?" we would not know how to answer.

—Parker Palmer

When Joseph Campbell described the journey of transformation, he
wrote of coming through the dark cave into a new springtime of
life. The important dimension he included is that when people come out of
pain into newness of life, they always bring an "elixir" or a gift with them.
This gift is meant not just for themselves, but for the transformation of the
world. So, too, with us. God is always extending compassion toward us,
loving us through the many ups and downs of our journey. We, in turn, are
meant to offer this compassion to others. Life is a constant cycle of giving
and receiving. The divine gift of love that we receive is meant to be shared.

I have come to see how my motivations for compassion are very significant. The more I am aware of my motivations, the more I can give the gift
of compassion with true freedom of heart, without any strings attached.
The freer I grow, the more genuine my generosity becomes. Like the lines
of the old song, "Freely, freely, I have received, freely, freely I give," so I can
offer compassion with a selfless approach when I am more conscious of my
reasons for giving.

If my motivations come out of "have to," guilt, self-affirmation, code-
pendency, a "fix-it" or problem-solving intention, or a "redeemer mentality,"
my compassion has too much of me in it and not nearly enough focus on
loving the one who hurts. The more I get to know my emotions, attitudes,
compulsions, and desires, the more transparent and truly compassionate I
will be. The healthier I am psychologically and spiritually, the freer I will be
in offering my gifts to others.

I have also discovered how essential it is to be compassionate toward
myself. The better I love myself, the better I can love others. Caregivers are

often great at extending the gift of compassion toward others, but do very poorly when it comes to extending that same compassion to themselves.

Gifts are meant to be given. Gifts are meant to be received. Gifts, true gifts, are offered freely. The question today is: how and why do I offer the gift of compassion?

THE DAILY PRACTICE

Breathprayer

> Breathing in: I receive . . .
> Breathing out: . . . I give

Reflection

> Hold your cup in your hands.
> Imagine the cup filled to the brim with God's endless compassion for you.
> Thank God for this gift.
> Take the cup and hold it up.
> Ask God to help you offer this compassion to others.
> Rest in the presence of God's love.

Scripture: Matthew 25:31-45

> For I was hungry and you gave me food.
> I was thirsty and you gave me something to drink.
> I was naked and you gave me clothing.
> I was a stranger and you welcomed me.
> I was sick and you took care of me.
> I was in prison and you visited me (Mt 25:35-36).

Journaling

> I usually extend compassion because . . .
> When I reflect on gifts being given, I . . .
> Thank you, God, for . . .

Prayer

God of compassion, take me to the ones who hurt.
May I see you in every face.
May I hear you in every voice.
May I welcome you in each relationship.
May I give freely with true generosity.

Today

I will choose an aspect of compassion that I need and give it to myself as well as to others.

Day 4

The Cup of Sacrifice

Compassion . . . is the strength that arises out of seeing the true nature of suffering in the world. Compassion allows us to bear witness to that suffering, whether it is in ourselves or others, without fear; it allows us to name injustice without hesitation, and to act strongly, with all the skill at our disposal.

—Sharon Salzberg

Compassion has a price. It does not come without a cost, the least of which is the pain that pierces our own hearts as we accompany one who is suffering. When we speak out and take a stand against injustice, our compassion can cost us ridicule, rejection, loss of friends, and even the termination of our job. When we are willing to be present with one who is in great physical or emotional pain, our compassion can cost us our precious time and energy. Sometimes when we suffer with others, such as the homeless, the dying, those with AIDS, the imprisoned, we can be confronted with our own fears, insecurities, powerlessness, arrogance, or prejudices.

Compassion urges us to move out of our comfortable niches of security. Compassion stretches us and asks us to let go of apathy and indifference. Compassion refuses to accept excuses of busyness, ignorance, or helplessness. Compassion invites us to reach out to those who suffer, "to live," as Sharon Salzberg notes, "with sympathy for all living beings without exception." Oh, how many times I wish that the "without exception" was not a part of the definition of compassion!

It can take many long years of living compassionately before we stop counting the cost and respond with fewer regrets or self-concerns. This is not to say that we omit taking care of ourselves or deny our own feelings. Far from it. It is the person who knows how to care well for self who will offer the purest and most generous compassion to another. We are, after all, to love others as we love ourselves (Lk 10:27).

When I think of the great sacrifice that compassion asks, I see Mary, the mother of Jesus, standing at the foot of the cross. She stood there bravely with the greatest sorrow a mother could have. Compassion cost Mary's son his life. Compassion cost Mary an agonizing grief that only a parent can fully realize. Both Mary and Jesus knew and paid the price of compassion.

THE DAILY PRACTICE

Breathprayer

> Breathing in: I stand . . .
> Breathing out: . . . beneath the cross

Reflection

> Stand with the cup in your hands.
> Visualize yourself with God's compassion filling your soul with love.
> Then picture someone (or a group) who hurts.
> Imagine what the pain must be like.
> Let your loving care and concern go to them.
> Stand at the foot of their cross.
> Send hope and courage to them.

Scripture: John 19:25-27

> Standing near the cross of Jesus were his mother, and his mother's sister, Mary the wife of Clopas, and Mary Magdalene . . . Jesus saw his mother and the disciple whom he loved standing beside her (Jn 19:25-26).

Journaling

> When I picture Mary, the mother of Jesus, standing at the foot of his cross, I . . .
> Here are some ways in which compassion costs me . . .
> Dear Mary . . .

Mary, woman of sorrows, your son's life was filled with compassion. Your life, too, teaches me to suffer with others even when it costs me to do so. May I be there at the foot of the cross of the suffering ones of this world in the loving way that you were at the foot of the cross of Jesus. May I learn from your love how to be a loving person.

Today

I will offer thanks for someone who paid a price for offering compassion to me. I will place myself beneath the cross of another who needs my compassion.

Day 5

Pouring from the Cup

Anyone who gives anything to the Divine will find that it comes back to them turned to gold.

—**Rumi**

Our lives are such that our deepest compassion and generosity often get masked by our frustration with schedules, calendars, and clocks. When this happens to me, I find myself becoming closed and selfish. Sometimes it takes a challenging or humbling moment to shake loose my tenacious hold on trying to get everything done on my carefully crafted timetable.

I am embarrassed to tell you about the following incident, but I will tell it because I learned a valuable lesson from it. One day, after being gone for three weeks, I returned home and found a huge heap of mail waiting for me.

I moaned and groaned, thinking of all the time it would take for me to open, process, and respond to what was there. In the pile of correspondence was an envelope with a cassette tape in it. There was no letter with it, and I could see from the return address that I did not know the person who had sent it. I felt irritated and impatient. I thought to myself, "Why did this person have to send a tape? It takes less time to read a letter than to listen to a tape."

I grouched and grumbled to myself for a day and then decided that I had better find out what was on that cassette tape. I discovered that it was sent by a blind woman. It contained one of the most beautiful letters I have ever received. I was deeply humbled and very regretful of my initial response. Here was a gift being given to me that I was ready to reject because I didn't want to take the time to listen to it. I was willing to pour out only a thimble-full of my time and attention for someone else while God was offering me a bushel-basket of golden insights and reflections.

Jesus encouraged his disciples toward generous loving and assured them that if they were generous in their giving, that this same generosity would be the measure of the gifts returned. Their giving would be turned to gold. Compassion is like that. When we let compassion pour forth generously from us instead of holding back with meager giving, it can be a powerful experience. We often receive more than we give.

Reflect today on your generosity and on God's. Have you had any life experiences when you hesitated or resisted giving and then, later, realized how much you had received in return?

THE DAILY PRACTICE

Breathprayer

> Breathing in: I give to you . . .
> Breathing out: . . . You give to me

Reflection

> Hold the cup in your hands.
> Look and see all the space it has for filling.
> Visualize God pouring love into your heart.
> Picture your heart filled with this love.

Bring to mind someone who is suffering.
Let the love within you go out to this person.
Picture your love poured out profusely, filling this person's whole being.
Sit in silence and be at peace.

Scripture: Luke 6:37-38

Give, and it will be given to you. A good measure, pressed down, shaken together, running over, will be put into your lap; for the measure you give will be the measure you get back (Lk 6:38).

Journaling

When someone is compassionate toward me, I . . .
God turned my giving into gold when . . .
One of the situations in my life where I tend to hold back and not offer compassion is . . . because . . .

Prayer

O God, you turn my meager offerings into golden treasures. Let me not be hesitant when you ask for my love in the form of compassion. You are so abundant in your compassion for me. May I be as generous with others. May the measure of compassion I give be the measure of compassion returned to me.

Today

I will pour generously from my cup of love and kindness today.

Day 6

The Gift of Be-ing

Just to be is a blessing,
Just to live is holy.

—Abraham Joshua Heschel

When I prepared for my first visit as a volunteer spiritual counselor at the hospice residence, I had planned to use guided imagery to help the patients relax and get in touch with their dying process. Well, that plan was short-lived. I quickly discovered that many of the men and women were very near death, usually too ill to focus, and sometimes in a near-coma stage. Once in a while they needed to talk through some of their fears and concerns, but usually they were very content for me to just be a hopeful presence, helping them know they were not alone.

I found that task much more difficult. I wanted to feel like I was "of use." Each time I left a patient, I wondered if the time had been worth it. "What am I *doing* there?" I'd ask myself. It took me many months before I could be at peace with just being there for each one. I now love to sit by the bedside of a dying person. I know that I receive as much as or more than I give. They help me face my own mortality and not to be afraid of death. It is such a special moment to be with someone in his or her final preparation for the mysterious journey to the other side of life.

We in the western world have been conditioned to think that it is only by our *doing* that we make a difference. We have to have something to show for our good intentions. While action is a vital part of Christian love, it has little effect unless there is a quality of "be-ing" with it. Sometimes the be-ing part of our care is what the other really needs. We may feel better if we *do* something like give a book to read, make a meal, or buy a gift, but maybe what they really long for is someone to simply sit and listen to their concerns.

When Jesus was in his excruciating moment in the Garden of Gethsemane, he needed his disciples to *be* with him while he prayed. He longed for the comfort of their presence and was pained by their inability to provide this for him. Jesus didn't need Peter to slice off an ear of his enemy. He just needed Peter and the others to be there with him as he faced his enemies (Lk 22:39-46).

A question that we often need to ask ourselves is: Can I trust myself, that I am enough, that I do not always have to be doing something to share my compassion?

THE DAILY PRACTICE

Breathprayer

Breathing in: Be-ing . . .
Breathing out: . . . be-ing

Reflection

Look at the cup before you.
Notice how simply it sits there but also how you are "with" the cup as you gaze upon it.
Intentionally recall the Divine Compassion within you.
Gather to your heart the pain of someone you know.
Be with this person and with the pain.
Do not try to "do" anything other than "be."
Be deeply and intimately bonded with this person.

Scripture: Matthew 26:36-46

Then Jesus said to them, "I am deeply grieved, even to death; remain here, and stay awake with me . . ." Then he came to the disciples and found them sleeping and he said to Peter, "So, could you not stay awake with me one hour?" (Mt 26:38, 41).

Journaling

The most difficult thing for me about "be-ing" with another who hurts is . . .
I remember when I needed someone to "be" with me . . .
Dear Compassionate One . . .

___

God of compassion,
When I hesitate to be with another, strengthen me.
When I question the quality of my presence, assure me.
When I want to show my worth through action, humble me.
When I miss the needs of the one who suffers, awaken me.
When I forget the beauty of a loving presence, remind me.
When I run away from the call to *be there*, bring me back.

Close by repeating this line several times:
"Just to be is a blessing."

Today
___

I will be present to another without charging into action.

Day 7

Integration/Review

1. Visit and review your past six days.

2. Highlight anything in your journal that particularly touches you with its truth.

3. Write a brief summary of this week. (Alternatives for this summary would be to use paints, clay, dance, or you could draw a cup and let the size, shape, form, contents, and message on it symbolize what you experienced this week.)

Memo

Are you growing concerned about "just one more week left?" Are you wondering if you have prayed these five weeks well enough? Are you doubting the value and worth of your daily practice? If you are, remember that prayer is not about progress and results or about feeling good. Prayer is about relating with God and having this relationship make a difference in the way we live our lives. Prayer is the intention of our hearts to commune with God. Renew that intention each day and let go of any anxiousness that you might have.

Week VI

THE BLESSING CUP

Day 1: The Blessing Cup
Day 2: The Memory Cup
Day 3: The Cup Brimming Over
Day 4: Disguised Blessings
Day 5: The Cup of Thanksgiving
Day 6: The Greatest Blessing
Day 7: Integration/Review

A View of the Week

Wherever you place your foot, there rests a blessing.

—Rumi

Perhaps the best known "cup" in the scriptures is that of the blessing cup in 1 Corinthians 10:16: "The blessing cup that we bless, is it not a sharing in the blood of Christ?" The cup of blessing is a term derived from the Jewish Passover rite, meaning not only that the cup is blessed, but also that the cup itself holds a blessing. It holds the gift of life.

Blessings. What are they? How do they come? What do they do for us? The dictionary defines blessing as: "to consecrate or to hallow by a religious rite or words; to make or pronounce holy or sacred." To bless is not so much to "make sacred," however, as it is to acknowledge the sacredness that is already there. All of creation is sacred because it is made by God. To bless anything of creation, be it a person or an object, is to acknowledge the touch of the Creator upon that person or object.

Wherever we place our feet—wherever we are—can be a blessing if we are aware of the inherent sacredness and beauty of that place. That "place" might be the heart of another person or the limb of a newly budded tree or a fuzzy caterpillar climbing a drainpipe. Attentiveness to the present moment is essential for a blessing to truly communicate the life and beauty of God to us. "Calling forth" a blessing is actually a naming of the goodness that is already there.

In the Hebrew scriptures, a blessing is perceived to be something that communicates divine life. With this life comes strength, stamina, and inner peace. Blessings or *berakahs* were often shared by the Jewish people. When they prayed "Blessed are you, O God . . ." they were acknowledging with gratitude all that God had done for them.

Blessings were given for a variety of purposes: to invoke divine care; to pray for someone; to regard another with favor; to bring happiness; to guard, preserve, protect, and to keep safe; to give good fortune or satisfaction; and to approve or encourage another. Whenever God blesses, there emerges bounteous life and an abundance of goodness. A prime example of this is in the twelfth chapter of Genesis when God blessed Abram and promised with the blessing that Abram would have many descendants, a symbol of the abundance of new life.

Anyone and anything that brings good or God-ness into our lives is a blessing. To bless is to bring the touch of God, the touch of love and good-ness, to another by our presence as well as by our actions. Blessings are a greeting from God, saying "I care about you. I desire what will be for your good. You are dear to my heart. I want your life to be filled with love."

Blessings are not always immediate, "feel-good" sorts of things. Some-times these blessings come disguised in the pain, struggle, and hardship of the unwanted parts of our lives. It is only later, with hindsight, that we look and see what a gift those times and events were for us.

As you pray through these days with the "blessing cup," may you grow in awareness of the countless blessings that are yours. May you become much more aware of how you yourself are a blessing in the lives of others by the loving quality of who you are and what you do. Most of all, may your love and appreciation for the Giver of all Gifts, the best of all blessings, continue to grow and be enriched.

Gifting God,

Tie a ribbon of remembrance
around my heart,
so that I can often recall
those sacred places
where you have made
yourself known in the
hidden recesses of my life.

Stir up my memory-cup,
let me look deeply within it,
seeing all the people and events
that have led me to you.

Refresh the photographs
of my mind
where the vivid traces
of your love
are etched
in our relationship,
and marked
upon my memory.

As I gaze into my
personal history
unlock the storage spaces
of my soul,
reveal the truth of your
bountiful love,
fill my heart
with awe and gratitude.

God of Beauty,
the blessing of your
loveliness
astounds my being,
the power of your
presence
enriches my every moment.
Blessed are you.
Blessed are you.

—**Joyce Rupp**

Day 1

The Blessing Cup

To bless is to put a bit of yourself into something. It is to make holy, to change something or someone because of your presence.

—Macrina Wiederkehr

It is not only ordained clergy who have the power or ability to bless. Each of us can offer blessings. Each of us can be a blessing, too. When we bless, it is God's deep and vast goodness, or God-ness, in us that blesses another. When we bless, we touch another with the touch of this God-ness. In the Christian scriptures, Jesus does not bestow or offer many blessings. Rather, he *becomes* a blessing. His presence, his goodness, engenders life, strength, healing, courage, and vitality.

Many, many people have blessed my life. Probably most of them are unaware of how they have done this unless I have deliberately thanked them for doing so. Usually they have blessed me by their smiles, their loving looks, their stories and affirmations, their concern and their care. Once in a while they also bless me with a formal blessing, one that includes special words and actions.

One such person who blessed my life in this way was an older woman named Emily, who was a member of my Servite community. I had been serving as Emily's retreat guide, and the last day that I met with her, I suddenly felt this urgent need to be blessed. I was just beginning the writing of my first book and the vulnerability and unanswered questions of that process were looming very large for me. I needed strength and encouragement. I had this sense that I ought to have my hands blessed.

Emily was very gracious. She took my hands in her own and held them, palms up, with great tenderness. I don't remember the words that she said. I recall only the profound sense of gratitude and peace that came over me at that time. I felt strength and courage well up in me. I knew then that not only did she believe in me, but that her goodness, her presence or God-ness was also blessing me. I left that place with renewed stamina and deepened hope, believing that the work I was about to do would be fruitful. Emily died of cancer several years after that blessing. I think of her often when I am using my hands for writing.

You may be at a place in your life where you can easily resonate with blessings, or you may be in a tough place where you wonder if you have ever blessed or been blessed. Wherever you are, I hope that you can pause today and believe in the possibility and the power of blessings.

THE DAILY PRACTICE

Breathprayer

> Breathing in: My God-ness . . .
> Breathing out: . . . blessing others

Reflection

> Hold the cup in your hands.
> Wrap your hands around the cup.
> Remember the God-ness dwelling within you.
> Think about people who have blessed you.
> How did they do this?
> Think about how you have blessed others.
> Give thanks for the God-ness in you.
> Give thanks for the ability to bless and be blessed.

Scripture: 1 Peter 3:8-12

> Repay with a blessing. It is for this that you were called—that you might inherit a blessing (1 Pt 3:9).

Journaling

> I experience my God-ness blessing others when I . . .
> These people have especially been a blessing for me . . .
> Blessed One . . .

Blessed are you, God, Source of all goodness. The boundless beauty and unlimited love of your presence bless me at every moment of my existence. May your goodness radiate from me and bring the blessing of your loving touch to each person with whom I share life.

Today

I will intentionally bless each person I meet today with the gift of my loving presence.

Day 2

The Memory Cup

Going from this place to another place is like the bird in winter who remembers the beauty of her Springtime nest just to keep herself from freezing.

—Nancy Wood

The gift of our memory is something we probably rarely think about until we get to the age where we have trouble remembering. Memory enables us to recall our blessings (our touches of God), to give thanks for them, and to grow because of them. Good memories can encourage us, warm us on a cold day, and help us to keep hope in our hearts. They serve as a way to keep us connected. Good memories can strengthen and sustain us.

As Christians we gather around a memory every time we meet to share the Eucharist. When Jesus blessed the bread and the cup of wine at the Passover meal (the Last Supper), he said to those who were dear to his heart, "Do this in remembrance of me" (Lk 22:19). The power of this story has remained to this day because of the way memory has carried it from one generation to another. The cup of wine has become a "memory cup," holding the story of One whose life was poured out all for humanity. It has become the cup of sacrifice, the cup of love, the cup of unity. This cup has given strength and restored hope to many a weary spiritual traveler.

Our ability to remember is a precious gift. It is in remembering our blessings that our hearts are filled with gratitude. Without memory we would be unable to savor the good things that have happened to us and for us. Without memory we would be unable to be healed from past painful situations. Memory can bless us or haunt us, depending on what stirs inside our mind and how we receive it and live with it.

We all have a wide variety of memories. Sometimes memories come forth that are not so pleasant for us. These memories may be asking for our attention. Perhaps they need to be dealt with and put to rest. Eventually we need to move on from our sad and distressing memories and focus on the memories that are consoling and strengthening for us.

Today, sift through your memories. Be the gatekeeper of these memories. Catch the ones that draw forth and enhance your core goodness. Savor them. Let these blessed memories fill you with hope.

THE DAILY PRACTICE

Breathprayer

> Breathing in: I remember . . .
> Breathing out: . . . your love for me

Reflection

> Hold the blessing cup in your hands.
> Let it be filled with memories.
> Choose one memory of love and happiness.
> Let this memory pervade your entire being.
> Receive the renewed inner strength it offers you.
> Write a word for this memory on a piece of paper.
> Place the word in your memory cup today.
> Thank God for this memory.

> But take care . . . so as neither to forget the things that your eyes
> have seen nor to let them slip from your mind all the days of
> your life; make them known to your children and your children's
> children (Dt 4:9).

Journaling

Go back to the memory that came to you as you prayed with the
memory cup. Write down any thoughts and feelings about this
memory that you want to store in your heart today.
How has this memory been a blessing for you?
Dear Bestower of Blessings . . .

Prayer

O Memory Giver, thank you for the storehouse of good memories
that is mine. May these blessed memories give me hope and
inspiration for my spiritual journey. I ask this day that the touch of
your goodness, your blessing, be with . . . *(name those you especially
want to bless)*. Thank you for your blessings.

Today

I will carry one blessed memory in my heart and let it sustain me
with happiness and peace.

Day 3

The Cup Brimming Over

You anoint my head with oil,
my cup brims over.

—Psalm 23:5

One time when I was four or five years old, I visited the home of my great-aunt Ida. I always looked forward to these visits because she was a wonderfully kind and generous woman. I can still see vividly how, on this particular day, she took her coin purse out, unzipped it, and put all the pennies it held into my hand. I don't remember how many pennies there were, but my small hand could hardly hold all of them. The bounty of those few pennies sent me into a tizzy of happiness.

I feel that same way with God's generosity to me. I am ever amazed at how God keeps on extending care and kindness to me no matter how I feel or think, no matter what mood I am in, no matter how loving or nasty I am. God keeps offering welcoming love and abiding peace to me. God is quite astounding. This Divine Being is a limitless lover, always filling the small hands of my life with grace and goodness, always enriching my life with all that I need for my spiritual path. In a way, God's love is like having a "bottomless cup." I can drink and drink from the abundance of God and there is still more love to be poured into my heart.

When I lean back and reflect upon the gifts I have in my life, I realize that the generosity of God is beyond my comprehension. Nothing I could ever do would "earn" all of these gifts that are freely and lavishly given. I marvel at the gift of my inner and outer life. I am astounded at the daily guidance I receive. I am in awe at the way the world works and at how the intricate human body restores and renews itself. I look at the universe and wonder who this Creating Power is to be so generous with colors, shapes, patterns, and designs. I remember the wonderful people who have come into my life, each with a unique gift to share with me, and I know without a doubt that through them I have been touched by Divine Love.

The scriptures often speak of the abundance of God. This divine love is described as being poured into our hearts (Rom 5:5). The book of Joel tells of God's Spirit being poured out on all humanity (Jl 2:28). The psalms use many images to proclaim the generosity of God's gifts. Our lives, too, are a testimony to the generosity of the Divine Giver. Today is a day to step inside the marvelous abundance of God and to enjoy what you find there.

THE DAILY PRACTICE

Breathprayer

> Breathing in: Brimming over . . .
> Breathing out: . . . with your love

Reflection

> Set your cup before you.
> Pour water into it so that it fills to the very brim, ready to wash over the edge.
> Sit and ponder how full the cup is.
> Close your eyes and picture God's love filling you.
> Let your entire being receive this love.

Scripture: Psalm 36:5-9

> How precious is your steadfast love, O God!
> All people may take refuge
> in the shadow of your wings.
> They feast on the abundance of your house,
> and you give them drink
> from the river of your delights (Ps 36:7-8).

Journaling

> My cup brims over when . . .
> I have difficulty receiving God's abundance when . . .
> Generous God . . .

Extravagant God,
Generosity beyond comprehension,
Bestower of all that I need,
Thank you for the immensity of your kindness.
Praise to you for the endless out-pouring of your love.
My being proclaims your goodness.

Today

As I pour liquids of any kind into a cup, a glass, or a bowl, I will smile inside as I remember how generous God is in filling my life with blessings.

Day 4

Disguised Blessings

In our sleep, pain that cannot forget
falls drop by drop upon the heart
and in our own despair, against our will,
comes wisdom through the awful grace of God.

—**Aeschylus**

Some of our greatest blessings have been difficult situations, uncomfortable ones we wanted to throw out of our lives as quickly as possible. Sometimes our greatest pain holds a gift for us that is hidden for a long, long time. The blessing is disguised amid the turmoil, confusion, heartache, and struggle. Sometimes we are unable to accept the blessing because we are still too hurt, too angry, too grieved, too overwhelmed, to receive it. It is only much later that we see the gift that has come from what we thought would destroy our happiness forever.

My brother David drowned at age twenty-three. I was twenty-five at the time. It was fifteen years before I found my gift amidst the grief. It was his death that led me to write about goodbyes, loss, and grief. It was my struggle with this catastrophe that helped me become the writer I am today. I would never say that my brother's death was a blessing, but I can now say that the insights and spiritual growth that eventually came out of that experience were blessings disguised within the sorrow.

Within each struggle, there is a blessing waiting to happen. The biblical passage of Jacob struggling with a messenger of God is a symbolic story of our own struggle with the unwanted parts of our life. All during the long night (the darkness), Jacob wrestles with this unknown figure (our unwanted life experiences). Jacob is wounded in the process (our memory of the experience). He is wise enough to say to the angel, "I will not let you go until you bless me." ("Give me some meaning, some hope, some wisdom from this inner wrestling match.") Jacob goes away limping but he is wiser than he was before the struggle began.

Sometimes the pain of our life doesn't make much sense but usually disguised blessings eventually come to light when we leave the fray behind and begin to let go of what has brought us so much misery. In the process of healing we begin to see the blessings that are ours. Today is a day to survey an experience that you wish you never had and see if there might be a blessing hidden within it.

THE DAILY PRACTICE

Breathprayer

Breathing in: Divine Wisdom . . .
Breathing out: . . . blessing me, blessing me

Reflection

Take your cup in your hands.
Stand and face the east, the direction of awakening, of insight, of new life.

Hold out your cup to God, the Wisdom-Giver.
Receive the wisdom from your disguised blessings.
Then hold the cup to your heart.
Stand for several minutes in quiet union with God.

Scripture: Genesis 32:22-32

Jacob was left alone; and a messenger of God wrestled with him until daybreak. When the messenger saw that he did not prevail against Jacob, he struck him on the hip socket; and Jacob's hip was put out of joint. . . . Then he said, "Let me go. . . ." But Jacob said, "I will not let you go until you bless me" (Gen 32:24-26).

Journaling

Something I wrestle with, try to make sense of, and wonder how it could ever contain a blessing is . . .
Some of my disguised blessings that I've gradually come to realize are . . .

All-knowing One, teach me . . .

Prayer

Holy Wisdom, come with your vast vision. Help me to sift through the rubble of my trying times, to find the teachings that can guide my life. You who see far beyond the devastation, lead me to believe that there might be gifts in what I want to toss away. I offer you my gratitude for all the disguised blessings that are mine.

Today

If an unwanted experience occurs today, I will not toss it out until I struggle to find a blessing in it.

Day 5

The Cup of Thanksgiving

For all of a sudden when I saw those lights, I said to myself...
this is your life, this is your real life, and you are living it. Your
life is not going to start later. This is it, it is now. It's funny
how a person can be so busy that they forget this is it. This is
my life.

—Lee Smith

A long time ago, I heard Jean Houston tell a story about herself as a
youth, going to hear a presentation by Helen Keller who was blind and
deaf. Houston said that after Helen Keller finished speaking, she knew that
she had to talk with her. She got up and presented her face to Helen Keller.
Jean Houston described the experience this way: "She read my whole face
and I blurted out: 'Miss Keller, why are you so happy?' and she laughed and
laughed, saying: 'My child, it is because I live each day as if it were my last
and life, with all its moments, is so full of glory."

It is amazing, isn't it, how we can miss so much of life? The key to
gratitude is surprise. When we lose our sensitivity to wonder and awe,
when we simply trudge or zoom through the days, we can so easily miss
the daily gifts of life. When we awaken to what is within us and around us,
when we savor, relish, and taste life fresh each day, our heart holds much
more gratitude for our blessings.

Andrew Harvey writes in *The Way of Passion* that if we were really looking at this world, we would be moved a hundred times a day by the flowers
at the side of the road, the people we meet, by all that brings us messages
of our own goodness and the goodness of all things. To be grateful is to
affirm goodness wherever we find it. The problem with being grateful is not
the lack of countless blessings; the problem is with being inattentive and
unaware of these blessings.

One practice that has helped to reawaken my gratitude when my thank-
fulness has grown lean is to take one of my five external senses each day
and be attentive to it. One day I notice all the sounds that I hear; another

day I pay close attention to everything I see, etc. Doing this helps me move out of my tired approach to life. I restore my alertness to my daily gifts and begin again to see the universe as one vast blessing.

Are you living your life right now? Or, are you still waiting for it to happen?

THE DAILY PRACTICE

Breathprayer

> Breathing in: Alive, aware . . .
> Breathing out: . . . thank you, thank you

Reflection: (using your five external senses to lead you to gratitude)

> Take your cup and place a favorite beverage in it.
> Listen to the sound of the liquid as you pour.
> Take the cup and smell the beverage.
> Look at the liquid, the color, fluidity, etc.
> Feel the liquid in the cup.
> Drink it very, very slowly. Taste it fully.
> Be aware of the blessing of your five senses.
> Give thanks.

Scripture: Psalm 116:12-19; Luke 22:14-23

> What return shall I
> make to God
> for all God's bounty
> to me?
> I will lift up the
> cup of salvation
> and call on the name of God (Ps 116:12-13).

> Then Jesus took the cup and gave thanks (Lk 22:17).

Journaling

I am most alert to my daily blessings when . . .
Something for which I am grateful, but rarely give thanks . . .
Thank you, Bountiful One . . .

Prayer

I thank you, God, with my whole heart,
I will tell of your wonderful deeds.
I will be glad and exult in you.
I will sing to you for you have dealt bountifully with me.
Your steadfast love endures forever (Ps 9:1-2; Ps 13:6; Ps
118:29).

Today

I will live this day as if it was my last.

Day 6

The Greatest Blessing

The finding is never complete. We can never know God exhaustively or completely. . . . But we can sometimes know. . . for sometimes we become so aware of the fierce beauty of God's light that it seems to be known because it is burning within us.

—Caryll Houselander

In *The House at Rest*, Jessica Powers has a marvelous poem in which she addresses God as a "God of too much giving." She then describes herself as getting inebriated with God. She is filled with overwhelming joy, because God has offered her "too many cups" of divine goodness. I think that the closest I ever came to being "drunk on God" was in my late twenties on my first visit to Switzerland. I remember sitting on top of one of the hills in the Alps and gazing in absolute awe at the immensity of the world. I was swept up in the beauty of God and the song "O God of Loveliness" kept resounding in my soul. The magnificence of it all was staggering.

God is, above all else, a being of immense beauty. It is this beauty that continues to draw us and enfold us in eternal goodness. This mysterious Beloved is forever wooing us, longing for us to be totally immersed in love of the purest kind. As I look at my life, I count as my greatest blessing the gift of God's own essence. Being able to know this wondrous God of beauty, being embraced and welcomed home time and again, all of this is truly powerful.

I see this immense goodness of God reflected in every variety of people and in all the facets of the universe that sing out the goodness of the Creator. Each one mirrors the essence of God's beauty. Each one is a vessel filled with manifestations of the Creator. I know this beauty, also, within myself, in the silent encounters deep within my own being. Every once in a while, each of us senses, for a moment, this rare blessing of the touch of God. Brief as it is, it is enough to remind us that there is an underlying harmony beneath all the chaos. There is an eternal beauty giving a loving texture to all of life.

Any and all experiences of God are pure gift. All moments of encounter with this Divine Beauty are given with unconditional love. As we end these six weeks, let us recall once more that we are in the embrace of a God of love who calls us "the Beloved," a God who is our "chosen portion and our cup" (Ps 16:5). Could we want for anything more?

THE DAILY PRACTICE

Breathprayer

Breathing in: God of beauty . . .
Breathing out: . . . Beloved One

Reflection

Put your hands around the cup.
Image yourself enfolded in God's hands.
Let the beauty of God sing in you.
Let the comfort of God wrap around you.
Let the goodness of God draw you closer.
Let the generosity of God open you to the world.
Let the love of God bring you peace.
Remain enfolded in this Eternal Beauty for as long as you can.

Scripture: Colossians 2:1-4; Romans 11:33-36

God's mystery . . . in whom are hidden all the jewels of wisdom and knowledge (Col 2:3).

Oh the depth of the riches and wisdom and knowledge of God! (Rom 11:33).

Journaling

The most wonderful thing about God is . . .
A listing of the ways I have particularly known the beauty of God . . .
God of loveliness, I . . .

___

Stand with arms outstretched and eyes wide open. Speak aloud all the names and qualities of God that come to your mind and heart. Let this be a litany of praise and thanksgiving for the gift of God in your life. When your litany is completed, fold your hands across your heart and bow your head in honor and reverence.

Today

___

I will place my hand over my heart, unite with God's beauty in my soul and in my world, and give thanks.

___

Day 7

Integration/Review

1. Visit and review your past six days.

2. Highlight anything in your journal that particularly touches you with its truth.

3. Write a brief summary of this week. (Alternatives for writing this summary would be to use paints, clay, dance, or you could draw a cup and let the size, shape, form, contents, and message on it symbolize what you experienced during the week.)

Memo

For the next week or so of your spiritual practice, you might want to review the entire six weeks that you have just completed. Pause at any of the places where you feel drawn to pray. Jot down any thoughts and feelings that you want to remember. Include them in your journal.

At the end of your review of the six weeks, you might want to draw a cup that expresses the awareness and revelations that you experienced over the six weeks of prayer. Another way to gather the highlights of the six weeks would be to write brief phrases on small pieces of paper and place these in your sacred cup. You could continue to be in touch with the graces of the six weeks by periodically drawing out one of the phrases, praying with it, and carrying it with you for a day.

Above all, I hope that you will be drawn many times to your relationship with God and the world whenever you use a cup or a vessel of any kind. May you keep returning to God through the common, ordinary reminders that are with you each day. May your thirst for God be strong enough to keep you faithful to a daily spiritual practice!

GROUP GATHERINGS

Editor's Note

In the process of writing *The Cup of Our Life*, the author, Joyce Rupp, worked with a group of men and women in Des Moines, Iowa. The individual members of the group used the book for prayer on a daily basis and then gathered at the end of the week to discuss their experiences and to pray together. The author found the process very helpful in preparing the final draft of the book.

As a result, *The Cup of Our Life* lends itself well for group use. For example, it can be used by groups that meet for prayer and/or bible study or as a follow-up to Renew programs, RCIA, retreats—any spiritual-growth group that meets regularly.

The following prayer services form the basis for group use of the book. Each service continues the week's theme and includes questions for sharing about the days of prayer. The process requires a leader to preside who can be any member of the group or someone who usually coordinates or facilitates the gathering. Allow at least an hour, perhaps more if necessary, for each group-centered reflection and discussion.

Information on the music mentioned in these services is given on page 163–167.

A Guide for Sharing in Group Gatherings

The following questions are suggestions for sharing your experience of each week. There are also specific questions for each week..

1. How would you summarize what you have learned from your days of spiritual practice during the past week?

2. As you reflect upon your week, which day was . . .
   your most insightful one?
   your most difficult one?
   your most quiet one?
   your most energizing one?

3. Did any questions arise that you would like to bring to the group discussion?

4. Is there anything else that you would like to bring to the group from your daily prayer?

A Note about Sharing

Please be sure to listen well to one another. Give every person in the group ample time and opportunity to speak before anyone speaks twice. Remember that sharing time is not problem-solving time. The purpose of the gathering is not to take care of anyone's difficulties; rather, it is a time to listen to one another and to encourage one another's spiritual growth by being present to and with one another.

Week I

The Cup of Life

Leader's Instructions

Place a glass pitcher filled with water and a lit candle next to the pitcher on a low table in the center of the group.

Invite the participants to introduce themselves and to share why they chose their particular cup for this prayer journey. After the introductions, the participants place their cups on the table. Continue with the following prayer.

Opening (Prayed Together)

Loving, life-giving God, you continuously pour your transforming love into the cup of our lives. Like a spring rain falling into the open soil, your love and ours is mixed and mingled into an energizing oneness. Your presence is the power we need to grow and to change. Your gift of love enables us to commit ourselves to the unending process of spiritual transformation. How grateful we are. How ready to grow!

Leader

Let us enter into quiet now as we focus on the life. of God within us.

Breathprayer

Breathing in: O Divine Life . . .
Breathing out: . . . streaming through me

After two or three minutes of quiet prayer, the group joins in a chant or a song ("In God We Live and Move" or "A Home In My Heart" from *Dear Heart, Come Home*, or "You Are a Love Song" from *Harvesting*).

O Divine Life, guide and direct our time of sharing. May we listen attentively to one another as we remember your presence within us and among us. Amen.

Sharing Time

(Refer to "A Guide for Sharing in Group Gatherings," page 140)

Other Questions

1. How do you feel about being God's love song? Does this thought influence how you live your life?

2. When are you most aware of God's dwelling within you? Within others?

3. How would you describe the experience of God's power working through you?

4. Do you have any difficulties with "boundaries" in relation to your spiritual practice? What kind of boundaries have you found helpful?

5. What is one way in which your cup was your teacher this week?

Closing

Read Together: John 4:10

The leader then takes the pitcher of water and holds it high as each of the participants holds out his or her hands toward the pitcher to bless the water.

Reader (group repeat after the reader)

May this water here before us
remind us of the vitality and vibrancy
of the Divine Presence within us.
May this water call us to be transparent

to allow the light of God to shine through us.
May the blessing of God be upon us
and upon this water
a source of life for us! Amen.

Leader

The leader then invites the participants to take their cups and hold them out to receive the blessed water. The leader pours a small portion of blessed water in each cup. When all cups have water in them, the group, including the leader, then lift the cups up as the leader proclaims:

Receive this blessed water.
May our drinking from these cups
refresh us in body and spirit.
(All then drink slowly and reflectively of the blessed water.)

Pray Together: The Prayer of Julian of Norwich

God, of your goodness, give me yourself,
for you are enough for me.
I can ask for nothing less
than what is completely to your honor,
and if I do ask for anything less,
I shall always be in want.
Only in you I have all.

Song

"My Soul Thirsts," Dan Schutte (or another song of your choice).

Blessings

Offer a sign of peace to one another. An alternative closing would be to lead the group in the following guided visualization, "Receiving the Cup." At the close, play the song, "You are a Love Song" and have the group listen to it.

Guided Visualization: Receiving the Cup

Go within . . . find a place that is quiet . . . safe, secure. . . . A small group of people comes to you. . . . They welcome you . . . they greet you with great affection . . . they take you into a forest. . . . As you walk with them, you come to a spring of water, a clear pool. . . . They ask you to wait there by the water . . . you look around and notice the beauty of the forest and the pool . . . then you see in the distance a Holy Guide coming to you. . . . The Guide greets you as a long, lost loved one. . . . The two of you find a place to sit down together by the pool of water. Sit quietly with the Guide for a few moments . . . (longer pause).

The Guide asks you about your life and listens to your responses:
What is your greatest joy now? . . . (longer pause).
What is your greatest difficulty? . . . (longer pause).
What is your deepest comfort? . . . (longer pause).

The Guide nods in understanding, truly hearing both your blessings and your struggles. . . . The Guide then gives you a wonderful cup . . . it is transparent, with beautiful etchings on it. . . . the light of the pool of water glistens through it. . . .

You receive the cup . . . hold it . . . look into it . . . and there you see something that has great significance for your life. . . . Ask the Guide to tell you about it, what it means for your life . . . (longer pause).

Keep holding the cup. The Guide motions for you to rise . . . and gives you a farewell embrace. . . . You take the cup with you and slowly you return with the gift that the cup holds for you. . . . Gather the cup to your heart and begin the journey home. . . . Slowly come back to this place and time. . . .

Week II

The Open Cup

Leader's Instructions

Place a lit candle in the center of the table with two cups next to it. One is sitting upright, open to receive. The other is turned upside down, unable to receive. Set all the participants' cups around the candle after completing the opening prayer.

Opening

Leader

Let us begin by holding our cups in our hands and looking into the open cup. Let us reflect on our inner world at this time: Is the cup empty? Half full? Filled to the brim? What more does the cup need? What does the cup need to pour out?

Leader (after a brief time of reflection)

I invite each of you to share one word, or a brief phrase, that tells what you see in your cup. (Just one word or phrase. There will be time for sharing more later on.) Pause for time to think of the word or phrase and then have the sharing of the word or phrase.

Chant

"I Open to You" or "Let Go, Come In" (from *Dear Heart, Come Home*) or "My Soul Thirsts" (from *Lover of Us All*).

Leader (after the chant)

O Divine Life, guide and direct our time of sharing. May we listen attentively to one another as we remember your presence within us and among us.

Sharing Time

(Refer to "A Guide for Sharing in Group Gatherings," page 140).

<u>Other Questions</u>

    1. What is some of your inner clutter?

    2. How do you experience "listening" in your prayer?

    3. Does the cycle of "emptying and filling" relate to your life experience?

    4. Describe what helps you to trust God.

    5. Have you been able to find solitude in your life?

Closing

The leader is sitting in the circle with the group. All sit with hands on laps, palms up, open and ready to both give and receive. The leader begins by proclaiming: "God, you are enough for me." Then each one in the circle also speaks the proclamation if she or he so chooses.

<u>Prayer for Openness</u>

Continue with "The Prayer for Openness." Go around the circle with each participant reading one of the sections. The last one is read by all in the group.

Spirit of freedom,
open my mind and my heart.
Lift the barriers,
unbind the strong grasp of my demands
when I want everything to go my way.

God of spaciousness,
reach into my inner space,
sweep out all the old clutter,
enlarge my capacity to receive.

Bringer of truth,
empty me of whatever impedes
the growth of our relationship.
Help me recognize and accept
your sources for my growth.

Creator of the seasons of life,
soften my resistance to emptying.
May I welcome each inner season
as a catalyst for my transformation.

Faithful Friend,
deepen my trust in you.
Ease my doubts, fears, and discouragements.
When I am feeling vulnerable,
remind me that you are my safe haven.

Divine Mystery,
may I be ever more rooted in you.
Draw me into solitude.
Entice me into endless encounters
where I experience oneness with you.

Holy Whisper,
open the ears of my heart.
May I hear your voice within the silence
as well as within the noise of my life.
Re-awaken me so that I can listen to you
wholeheartedly.

Bringer of Good and Giver of Growth,
we yearn to be open and receptive
to your generosity.
May we trust your presence amidst the cycle
of emptying and filling.

Song

Listen to the song "God is Enough" (from *Her Wings Unfurled*) or
another song.

Go to each one in the group and bless one another with these words: "May God be enough for you."

Week III

The Chipped Cup

Leader's Instructions

Place a lit candle in the center of the table. Around it, set up several items that are in less-than-perfect condition. For example, you can use a partially burned candle; a chipped or cracked cup, dish, or plate; a frayed or stained dishcloth or towel; a torn or wrinkled book jacket; a leaf with a hole in it or some spots on it; or a tarnished piece of silverware.

Opening

Invite each person to come forward and place his or her cup on the table with the less-than-perfect items. As the cup is placed, the person says his or her name. After all the cups are on the table, the group extends their hands over the cups as the leader prays:

Leader

Loving Creator, we come to you with our strengths and our weaknesses, with our light and dark sides. We ask your blessing to be upon us and these cups with which we pray each day. May we accept and love ourselves while we also stretch and grow into ever greater wholeness.

<u>*Breathprayer (Continue with Breathprayer for two to three minutes)*</u>

Breathing in: You, in me . . .
Breathing out: . . . I, in you

<u>*Chant*</u>

"Lead Me In Your Love" (from *Dear Heart, Come Home*).

Turn to the poem at the beginning of Week III on page 54. Go around the circle, with each individual reading one section of the poem. All read the last section together.

<u>*Leader*</u>

O Divine Life, guide and direct our time of sharing. May we listen attentively to one another as we remember your presence within us and among us. Amen.

Sharing Time

(Refer to "A Guide for Sharing in Group Gatherings," page 140.)

<u>*Other Questions*</u>

1. Does "perfectionism" influence your life with God?

2. What have you learned about your Shadow?

3. Who has taught you about mercy?

4. Do you find your spiritual path affected by the expectations of yourself or others? If so, how?

5. How do you search for wisdom in your life?

Closing

Sit in a circle, if not already doing so.

Song

"We Bring Who We Are" (from *Dancing Sophia's Circle*); or "All Shall Be Well" (from *Light of Christ*); or "A Time of Love" (from *Companion God*).

Sharing Strengths and Weaknesses

The leader invites the members of the group to reflect on their inner strengths. Then the leader asks each member to name one of his or her strengths (just one or two words from each person as they go around the circle). No comments are made after each sharing. Each strength is received in silent respect.

When the strengths have been shared, the leader then invites the members of the group to reflect on their weaknesses ("chips" or "flaws"). Then, the leader invites each member to share one of his or her weaknesses. No comments are made after each sharing. Each weakness is received in silent respect.

The group now stands in a circle, holding hands. Going around the circle, the total group speaks the following to each member of the group. As they do so, they look with love and acceptance upon the one to whom they are speaking:

"*(Name of the person being addressed)*, you are the beloved of God."

Blessings

Close with giving individual blessings or a sign of peace to one another.

Week IV

The Broken Cup

Leader's Instructions

Place a cup, a lit candle, and a cross in the center of the table. Scatter some Band-Aids around the table, one for each person present.

Opening

The leader invites the group to imagine being sheltered under the wings of God. Take one or two minutes to sit quietly under the wings of God. Then, chant "Shelter Me" (from *Dear Heart, Come Home*) or sing "Do Not Fear to Hope" (from *Do Not Fear to Hope*).

The leader invites each person to come forward and take a Band-Aid from the table.

All sit quietly and reflect upon any wound or hurt that needs healing in themselves or in someone they know. Allow several minutes to pray silently for healing of this wound. Then invite participants to place a Band-Aid on their own cup.

Chant

Repeat the chant, "Shelter Me," several times.

Leader

O Divine Life, guide and direct our time of sharing. May we listen attentively to one another as we remember your presence within us and among us. Amen.

Sharing Time

(Refer to "A Guide for Sharing in Group Gatherings," page 140.)

<u>Other Questions</u>

    1. When have you felt like a broken cup?

    2. What form have some of your resistances to God taken?

    3. Describe a time when you were healed of an inner wound.

    4. Do you think that there is such a thing as an "unmendable cup"?

    5. What form of prayer is most helpful for you when you are feeling wounded?

Closing

Each participant holds his or her cup. The leader gives each a slip of paper. Each one writes his or her name on the paper. Then the paper is placed inside of the cup as a sign of being hidden and sheltered by God. During the time when the names are being written, the song "Rest In My Wings" (from *Cry of Ramah*) could be played.

<u>All Pray: Psalm 32:7</u>

You are a hiding place for me;
you preserve me from trouble;
you surround me with glad cries of deliverance.

<u>Psalm Verses</u>

Continue with the following psalm verses, going around the circle or alternating with the leader:

Be merciful to me, O God, be merciful to me,
for in you my soul takes refuge;
in the shadow of your wings I will take refuge,
until the destroying storms pass by (Ps 57:1).

O my strength, I will watch for you,
O my strength, I will sing praises to you,
for you, O God, are my fortress,
the God who shows me steadfast love (Ps 59:9, 17).

Let me abide in your tent forever,
find refuge under the shelter of your wings (Ps 61:4).

For you, O God, are my hope,
my trust, O God, from my youth.
Upon you I have leaned from my youth (Ps 70:5-6).

I would feed you with the finest of wheat,
and with honey from the rock I would satisfy you (Ps 81:16).

You who live in the shelter of the Most High
who abide in the shadow of the Almighty
will say to God: "My refuge, my fortress;
my God in whom I trust" (Ps 91:1-2).

God is your keeper;
God is your shade at your right hand.
God will keep your going out
and your coming in
from this time and forevermore (Ps 121:5, 8).

As the mountains surround Jerusalem,
so God surrounds the people,
from this time on and forevermore (Ps 125:2).

Let me hear of your steadfast love
in the morning,
for in you I put my trust.
Teach me the way in which I should go,
for to you I lift up my soul (Ps 143:8).

God heals the brokenhearted
and binds up their wounds (Ps 147:3).

Stand in a circle, holding hands. The leader brings the cross from
the table and passes it around the circle. As each one holds the cross,
he or she names someone who is wounded and in need of healing.

Leader:

Blessed are you, Healing God. Your shelter is always with us. Mend those we have named this evening. May we each bring your healing love to those with whom we live and work by the power of your presence shining through us. Blessed are you, Healing God, blessed are you. Amen.

Blessings

Turn to one another and bless one another by making the Sign of the Cross on one anothers' foreheads and offering a word of support and encouragement.

Week V

The Cup of Compassion

Leader's Instructions

Place a lit candle in the center. Cover the table with magazine and newspaper photos of people throughout the world.

Opening

Begin by singing one of these songs about the Body of Christ: "We Are the Body of Christ" (from *Cry of Ramah)*; "We Are The Body of Jesus" (from *Nothing Without Love)*; or "Song of the Body of Christ" (from *Table Songs)*.

The group then stands, holding their cups in their hands. Begin by facing the east. Stand silently, cups held out to the people of the east. After a moment's silence, all say: "We are the Body of Christ." Turn, face the south, and do the same. Continue with the directions of the west and the north.

"A Prayer of Compassion"

Be seated and pray the following prayer. The prayers can be prayed by going around the circle or they can be prayed alternately with the leader. All pray the last section together.

We walk with others who hurt and ache. As we do so, keep us closely united with you, Healing Presence, so that our hearts will always be warm with compassion.

We walk with ourselves in our own joys and sorrows. May we look upon our own selves with love, with a belief that we, too, need tending and care.

We walk with our families, communities, loved ones and friends. Our hearts can be closely connected in good times and in bad.

May we draw strength from you and be open to the ways in which you call us to be there for them.

We walk with our world, a world that is filled with pain and grief, with beauty and grandeur. We are all children of the universe. Remind us that who we are and what we do affects our brothers and sisters, the earth, and all creatures in any form.

We walk with wounds yet to be healed. Do not let us run from what we need to face. Grant us the courage to let go of whatever keeps us from being healed. Help us to trust you with our lives, God.

We walk with scars that tell of the tough times we have had. Our wounds can be our teachers. God of wisdom, draw us to quiet times of reflection so that we can see and accept the truths that our wounded times have offered to us.

We walk in your presence, God. May our inner vision keep us closely bonded with you. Assure us often that we are all a part of the Body of Christ. When we meet another, we meet you. May the treasure of our union with you energize us and renew us as we reach out to others. Amen.

(Place all of the cups on the table at this time.)

Leader

O Divine Life, guide and direct our time of sharing. May we listen attentively to one another as we remember your presence within us and among us. Amen.

Sharing Time
(Refer to "A Guide for Sharing in Group Gatherings," page 140.)

Other Questions

1. Who are some of the people who have been your teachers of compassion?

2. Does the "Body of Christ" influence your spiritual path in any way? If so, how?

3. What are some of your motivations for being compassionate?

4. How has compassion cost you?

5. Share a situation in which you struggled with "being and doing."

Closing

"Just to Be" (from *Dancing Sophia's Circle*) or a song about the Body of Christ.

Guided Visualization

The leader should read the following to the group:

See yourself by the shore of the Sea of Galilee. . . . Jesus comes to you . . . the two of you sit down together. . . . Jesus looks upon you with great love. . . . Receive this love. . . .

Then Jesus blesses you: he places his hands on your head and says to you: "Receive the gifts of the mind." Receive these gifts. . . .

Jesus places his hands on your ears: "Receive the gift of listening clearly and with love." Receive this gift. . . .

Jesus places his hands on your eyes: "Receive the gift of seeing deeply." Receive this gift. . . .

Jesus places his hands on your mouth: "Receive the gift of speaking kindly and justly." Receive these gifts. . . .

Jesus places his hands on your heart: "Receive the gifts of compassion and forgiveness." Receive these gifts. . . .

Jesus places his hands on your feet: "Receive the gift of going to those in need." Receive this gift. . . .

Then, Jesus holds your hands and says to you: "These hands are made for both giving and receiving. . . ." He lifts your hands and kisses each one of them. . . . He looks into your eyes and says to you: "The gift you have received, give as a gift. . . ."

Thank Jesus for his presence and his gifts. . . . Then return to this time and place with the gifts you have received. . . .

Closing

Stand in a circle, joining hands. Each one calls out the gift(s) he or she desires to share with the hurting ones of the world.

Conclude by chanting "Lead Me In Your Love" (from *Dear Heart, Come Home*).

Week VI

The Blessing Cup

Leader's Instructions

Place a lit candle and a vase of fresh flowers (one flower for each person present) in the middle of the table.

Opening

Breathprayer

Breathing in: Generous God . . .
Breathing out: . . . thank you

Chant

"Beautiful Beloved" (from *Dear Heart, Come Home*).

The leader reads the first section and then others continue, going around the circle. All pray the last section together.

Generous God, you have poured so much into our blessing cups. You have offered us many graced moments filled with wonders of your goodness. You have been bountiful in sharing your presence of unconditional love with us.

All-embracing God, you call us to share our cup of compassion with those who are searching, suffering, and sorely in need of our hospitality. You daily invite us to be in union with all those you have created and gathered to your heart.

Healing God, you know how our lives each have their share of heartaches and brokenness. You see the deepest recesses of our spirits where pain and confusion need the touch of your restoring power. Remind us often that broken hearts can be healed.

Perceptive and insightful God, you see into the cup of our hearts. You know where the clutter lies. You invite us daily to pour out all that keeps us from being truly focused on communion with you. Again and again, you whisper to us, "Empty, pour out, let go of all that keeps you from being your true self."

Ever-present and understanding God, you have created us as fully human persons. Our cup of life bears chips, stains, and cracks as does our own personality and life-story. You encourage us to see the stains as a way to our transformation. You offer us wisdom and guidance to know when the cup needs to be washed and scrubbed and when the stains need to be lovingly accepted.

Forgiving God, you know our weaknesses and failures. There are times when we resist what you desire to pour into the cup of our life. You know how we ignore or refuse to be open and receptive. Yet, you continue to believe in us. You are always waiting, ready to fill our cup with your generous love.

Gifting God, the contents of the cup are meant to refresh, nourish, and renew life. You call us to bless others with our cup of life. Stir up within us a desire to offer our gifts to those who need them.

Loving, life-giving God, you continuously pour your transforming love into the cup of our life. Like a spring rain falling into the open soil, so your love and ours is mixed and mingled into an energizing oneness. Your presence is the power we need to grow and to change. Your blessing of love enables us to commit ourselves to the unending process of spiritual transformation. How grateful we are! How ready to grow!

Song

"Here Is the Cup," Joyce Rupp, page 163.

Leader

O Divine Life, guide and direct our time of sharing. May we listen attentively to one another as we remember your presence within us and among us. Amen.

Sharing Time

(Refer to "A Guide for Sharing in Group Gatherings," page 140.)

Other Questions

1. Of the blessings in life that you have received, which one means the most to you?

2. What quality of God touches your life greatly?

3. Describe your favorite memory of something or someone who helped you to grow spiritually.

4. Share one of your disguised blessings.

5. What helps you to be aware of and alert to your daily blessings?

Closing

Song

"The Name of God" (from *As Water to the Thirsty*).

Pray Together: Psalm 116:12-13

What shall I return to God
for all God's bounty to me?
I will lift up the cup of salvation
and call on the name of God.

Blessing

Pause to think about what blessing you most want to share with each one in the group. You have journeyed together for six weeks. You have heard one another's joys and sorrows. What blessing do you want give? Mentally and heartily put this "blessing" in your cup. Then, go to the others in the group and take turns pouring your blessings upon one another. Do this by lifting your cup over the head of another person and "pouring out" the blessing as you speak your blessing to him or her.

Song

"Pilgrim Companions" (from *Drawn by a Dream*) or another song of praise and thanksgiving.

Here is the Cup

Joyce Rupp

As Water to the Thirsty, David Haas
GIA Publications
7404 S. Mason Ave.
Chicago, IL 60638
708-496-3800

Cry of Ramah, Colleen Fulmer
The Loretto Spirituality Center
725 Calhoun St.
Albany, CA 94709
415-525-4174

Dancing Sophia's Circle, Colleen Fulmer
The Loretto Spirituality Center
725 Calhoun St.
Albany, CA 94709
415-525-4174

*Dear Heart, Come Home, Chants
and Visualizations,* Joyce Rupp
Crossroad Publishing Co.
370 Lexington Ave.
New York, NY 10017
212-532-3650

Do Not Fear to Hope, Rory Cooney
OCP
5536 NE Hassalo
Portland, OR 97213
800-548-8749

Drawn by a Dream, Dan Schutte
OCP
5536 NE Hassalo
Portland, OR 97213
800-548-8749

Her Wings Unfurled, Colleen Fulmer
The Loretto Spirituality Network
725 Calhoun St.
Albany, CA 94709
415-525-4174

Harvesting, Theresa Hucal
The Sisters of Charity
Box 2266
Saint John, New Brunswick
Canada E2L3V1

Light of Christ, Rufino Zaragoza
OCP
5536 NE Hassalo
Portland, OR 97213
800-548-8749

Lover of Us All, Dan Schutte
OCP
5536 NE Hassalo
Portland, OR 97213
800-548-8749

Nothing Without Love, Kathy Sherman, C.S.J.
Sisters of St. Joseph
1515 W. Ogden Ave.
LaGrange Park, IL 60525
312-354-9200

Table Songs, David Haas
GIA Publications
7404 S. Mason Ave.
Chicago, IL 60638
708-496-3800

Bibliography

Borg, Marcus. *Meeting Jesus Again for the First Time: The Historical Jesus and the Heart of Contemporary Faith*. San Francisco: HarperSanFrancisco, 1994.

Bruteau, Beatrice. *Radical Optimism: Rooting Ourselves in Reality*. New York: Crossroad, 1993.

Bruteau, Beatrice. *The Easter Mysteries*. New York: Crossroad, 1995.

Chodron, Pema. *Start Where You Are: A Guide to Compassionate Living*. Boston: Shambhala, 1994.

Fulghum, Robert. *From Beginning to End: The Rituals of Our Lives*. New York: Villard Books, 1995.

Griffin, Emilie. *Turning*. New York: Doubleday, 1982.

Hammarsjkold, Dag, (translated by: W. H. Auden & Leif Sjoberg). *Markings*. London: Faber and Faber, 1964.

Hart, Louise. *On The Wings of Self-Esteem*. Berkeley, CA: Celestial Arts, 1994.

Harvey, Andrew. *The Way of Passion: A Celebration of Rumi*. Berkeley, CA: Frog, Ltd., 1994.

Hay, Louise. *You Can Heal Your Life*. Carlsbad, CA: Hay House, 1994.

Hillisum, Etty. *An Interrupted Life: Diaries of Etty Hillisum*. New York: Washington Square Press, 1981.

Houselander, Caryll. *The Reed of God*. London: Sheed and Ward, Ltd., 1976.

Hucal, Theresa. *Harvesting: Songs of Theresa Hucal*. New Brunswick, Canada: Sisters of Charity, 1987.

Kornfield, Jack. *A Path With Heart: A Guide through the Perils and Promises of Spiritual Life*. New York: Bantam Books, 1993.

Jones, Laurie Beth. *Jesus, C.E.O.: Using Ancient Wisdom for Visionary Leadership*. New York: Hyperion Press, 1995.

Lamott, Anne. *Bird by Bird: Some Instructions on Writing and Life*. New York: Doubleday, 1994.

L'Engle Madeleine. *Walking on Water: Reflections on Faith and Art*. Gross Pointe Park, MI: Shaw Books, 2001.

Meadows, Mary Jo. *Gentling the Heart: Buddhist Loving-Kindness Practice for Christians*. New York: Crossroad, 1994.

Merton, Thomas. *New Seeds of Contemplation*. New York: New Directions, 1961.

Miller, William. *Make Friends with Your Shadow*. Minneapolis: Augsburg, 1981.

Moyne, John, and Coleman Barks. *Open Secret: Versions of Rumi*. Putney, VT: Threshold Books, 1984.

Muller, Wayne. *Legacy of the Heart: The spiritual advantages of a painful childhood*. New York: Simon & Schuster, 1992.

Julian of Norwich, (trans. by M. L. del Mastro). *Revelations of Divine Love*. New York: Doubleday, 1977.

Nouwen, Henri J. M. *Can You Drink the Cup?* Notre Dame, IN: Ave Maria Press, 1996.

Nouwen, Henri J. M. *Life of the Beloved: Spiritual Living in a Secular World*. New York: Crossroad, 1996.

Oliver, Mary. *New and Selected Poems*. Boston: Beacon Press, 1992.

Palmer, Parker J. *The Active Life: Wisdom for Work, Creativity, and Caring*. San Francisco: HarperSanFrancisco, 1990.

Powers, Jessica. *The House at Rest*. Peawaukee, WI: Carmelite Monastery, 1984.

Remen, Rachel Naomi. *Kitchen Table Spirituality: Stories That Heal*. New York: Riverhead Books, 1996.

Salzberg, Sharon. *Loving-Kindness: The Revolutionary Art of Happiness*. Boston: Shambhala, 1995.

Sarton, May. *Journal of a Solitude*. New York: W.W. Norton, 1973.

Sarton, May. *Selected Poems*. New York: W.W. Norton, 1978.

Siegfried, Regina, Robert Morneau, (eds.). *Selected Poetry of Jessica Powers*. Kansas City, MO: Sheed and Ward, 1989.

Smith, Lee. *Fair and Tender Ladies*. New York: Ballantine Books, 1988.

Tagore, Rabindranath. *Gitanjali: A Collection of Indian Songs*. New York: Macmillan, 1971.

de Waal, Esther. *Every Earthly Blessing: Celebrating a Spirituality of Creation*. Ann Arbor, MI: Servant Publications, 1991.

Weber, Christin Lore. *The Finding Stone*. San Diego: Lura Media, 1995.

Weems, Ann. *Psalms of Lament*. Louisville, KY: Westminster John Knox Press, 1995.

Wicks, Robert. *Seeds of Sensitivity*. Notre Dame, IN: Ave Maria Press, 1994.

Wiederkehr, Macrina. *Song of the Seed: A Monastic Way of Tending the Soul*. San Francisco: HarperSanFrancisco, 1995.

Wiederkehr, Macrina. *A Tree Full of Angels: Seeing the Holy in the Ordinary*. San Francisco: Harper & Row, 1988.

Wood, Nancy. *Dancing Moons*. New York: Doubleday, 1995.

Other Works by Joyce Rupp

Books from Ave Maria Press:

The Circle of Life

Fragments of Your Ancient Name

Fresh Bread

Inviting God In

May I Have This Dance?

May I Walk You Home?

May You Find Comfort

May You Rejoice

Now That You've Gone Home

Open the Door

Out of the Ordinary

Prayers to Sophia

Praying Our Goodbyes

Rest Your Dreams on a Little Twig

The Star in My Heart